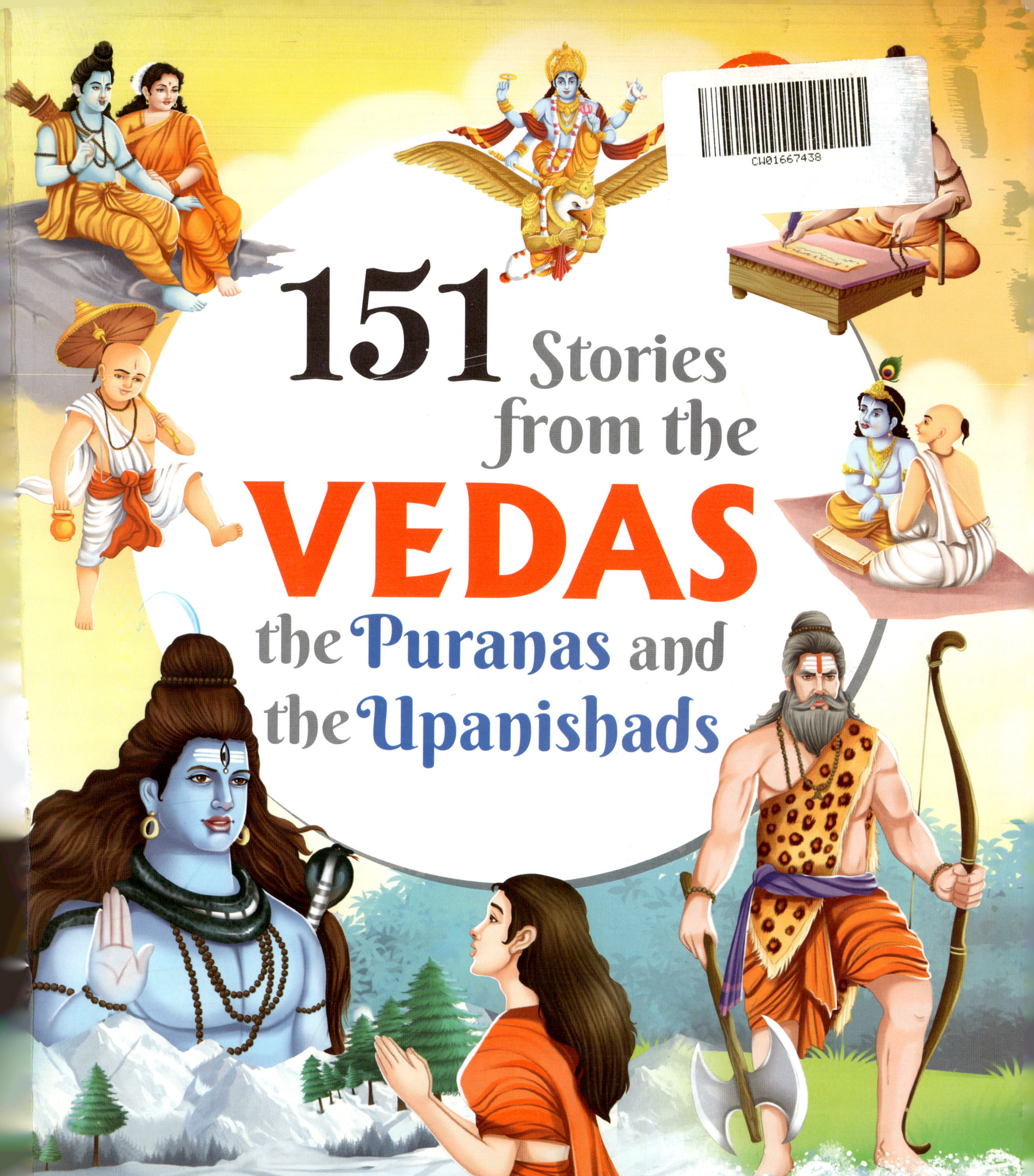

151 Stories from the VEDAS the Puranas and the Upanishads

MANOJ PUBLICATIONS

151 Stories from the Vedas, the Puranas and the Upanishads

Publisher:
MANOJ PUBLICATIONS
761, Main Road, Burari, Delhi-110084 (INDIA)
Mobile : 09999476076, 9868112194,
8178823569, 8178854810
E-mail : info@manojpublications.com
For online shopping visit our website:
www.sawanonlinebookstore.com

ISBN : 978-93-6270-580-8

CONTENTS

1. *The Vedas*

The Vedas are generally known as the scriptures of the Hindu community. The Vedas, the collection of mantras, are of four types, namely the Rig Veda, the Yajur Veda, the Sama Veda, and the Atharva Veda with the Rig Veda being the oldest. The Vedas have been divided into four styles of text – the Samhitas (mantras), the Brahmanas (text on rituals, ceremonies and sacrifices), the Aranyakas (commentaries on rituals) and the Upanishads (text related to meditation). The four stages of human life are the focus of each of these divisions.

The Rig Veda mantras, comprising stanzas of verses, are called 'Rik' and rely on their pronunciation, conveying a wrong meaning when not followed. It is a collection of poems, prayers and songs sung by the Aryans mainly in praise of Nature and its bounty, in all its various expressions. The Sama Veda consists of 'Saman' or chantings, arranged as a musical score, while the Yajur Veda is full of 'Yajus' or 'mantras meant for sacrifice'. Unlike the other three Vedas, the Atharva Veda is not so concerned with sacred rituals, but addresses the daily problems of Vedic people.

2. *The Creation of the Universe*

The Vedas are the holy texts of Hinduism. Sanatan Dharma (Hinduism) believes that the Vedas have always existed and have neither beginning nor end. The Vedas were not revealed to a certain person at a specific historical moment. They were apprehended by sages in deep meditation. Everything was covered in darkness at first. Behind this darkness lay water. In the sea, the gods gathered together. They pulled the Sun out of the ocean. Heaven and Earth were created by them.

In the beginning, the Vedas existed in oral form. The Rishis taught them orally. The Vedas are, therefore, regarded as Shruti in Hinduism meaning "what is heard". They were written between 1500–500 BCE (the so-called Vedic Period) in India. *Bhurja Patra* (birch leaves) and *Tada Patra* (palm leaves) were flattened and used as paper. Then the Vedas were written on these leaves and tied together as Punthis or Pothis.

3. *Vedavyasa*

Once upon a time, there was a sage called Maharshi Parashara. He was the author of the first ever Purana - The Vishnu Purana. One fine morning, when he was travelling near the river Yamuna, he saw a young woman, Satyawati, also known as Matsyagandha due to the fishy smell that came out of her body. Maharshi Parashara married Matsyagandha. She gave birth to a boy who was later known as Vedavyasa. Since Vyasa was born on an island, he was also called Krishna Dwaipayana, or the 'dark one' of the island. As he grew, he showed great interest in scriptures. The Atharva Veda was the only Veda in existence at the time. Krishna Dwaipayana divided this Veda into Rig, Sama, Yajur and Atharva Vedas so that it became easy for people to understand. As a result, Krishna Dwaipayana was known as Vedavyasa, or 'Splitter of the Vedas'. He also wrote the Mahabharata.

4. *The Supreme Entity and the Vedic Mantra*

The Vedas acknowledge the existence of a Single, Eternal Being that exists beyond and above everything. According to the Rig Veda, there is only one God (Eka Eva), who has created various gods and given them various names. The Atharva Veda confirms the existence of a Single Entity. The Yajur Veda goes on to say that this Single Entity is a friendly one. The Gayatri Mantra from the Rig Veda is considered to be the most powerful of all Vedic mantras. The mantra is extracted from the 10th verse of Hymn 62 in Book III of the Rig Veda.

"Om bhur bhuvah svah tat savitur varenyam
bhargo devasya dhimahi
dhiyo yo nah prachodayat."

It means–Let us meditate on that excellent glory of the Divine Light (Sun). May He stimulate our understanding (knowledge, intellectual illumination)!

5. *The Abode of the Vedic Gods*

It was believed that the gods' habitat, or place of residence, was significantly higher than that of humans. It was the mountains and the sky. People could only gaze up at the enigmatic skies and distant mountain tops from the surface of the Earth below. They were astonished beyond belief. Thus, they believed those enigmatic and magnificent locations to be the homes of strong beings that were superior to them.

The deep sea was a mystery or wonder, of course. What exactly was inside was beyond human comprehension. It was, therefore, believed that certain gods lived in the sea.

Loka means place, and Dyu means sky. Dyuloka, then, means the gods' sky-place.

6. Vedic Gods – Indra and Varuna

Indra is the most popular and praised god in the Vedas. He is the lord of the heavens. He is the god of thunder and rain and a great warrior. His Vahan is a white elephant called Airavata and has a weapon of lightning called Vajrayudh, also known as vajra.

Varuna is the defender of law and order in this world. He has supreme knowledge and knows everything happening in this world. He is the world's guardian. He watches over the entire world with a thousand eyes. The Vedas call him 'Samrat'. He punishes those who break the law but forgives them out of compassion if they repent and pray. By activating Vayu, the lord of the wind, he sustains life by giving rain and crops. He is portrayed as having four hands and riding chariots drawn by seven swans.

7. Agni and Vayu

Agni is the master of sacrifices and wealth. No sacrifice is complete without his presence. He is portrayed as having 2 heads, 6 eyes, 7 hands, 3 legs and 4 horns with a pot belly and long flowing hair. Agni has many names: Vahni (The one who receives the hom, or burnt sacrifice); Vitihotra (The one who sanctifies the worshipper); Dhananjaya (The one who conquers riches); Jivalana (The one who burns); Dhumketu (whose sign is smoke); Chhagaratha (The one who rides a ram); Saptajihva (The one who has seven tongues).

Vayu is the lord of beauty and intelligence. He is also called the lord of thoughts. He is considered to bring light to the earth and heaven. He is depicted as being blue in colour with four hands. Two of the hands hold a fan and a flag respectively while the other two hands are in abhaya and varada mudras.

8. *Surya, Vishnu and Mitra*

Surya is the lord of light and power. He is depicted as being golden with radiant hair. He is seen riding swiftly across the sky in his golden chariot drawn by 7 horses. Surya and Savitri or Savitr are two names by which the Sun is commonly addressed in the Vedic hymns.

Vishnu is the protector of people. He upholds the threefold existence, i.e. heaven, the earth and the living creatures. It is said that his incarnation 'Vamana' covered both heaven and the earth in two steps and crushed demon Bali in the third step.

Mitra is also the guardian of the world along with Varuna. Mitra is associated with the morning light while Varuna is associated with the night sky. In the Rig Veda, the oldest of the Vedic texts, Mitra is mostly indistinguishable from Varuna, together with whom Mitra forms a dvandva pair Mitra-Varuna.

9. *The Ashvini Kumaras*

The Vedic goddess of the clouds and morning light, Saranyu, also known as Sanjna, had abandoned her husband, the Sun-god, because she was unable to bear his heat and brilliance. She assumed the shape of Ashvini, a mare, and was content to graze in far-off fields. However, the Sun discovered her and won her over once more. Two more children were born to them. They were identical twins. They were called Ashvini Kumaras. They are represented as humans with the heads of a horse. They are divine healers and frequently saved both gods and humans. They travel in a chariot with three spokes. The Rig Veda compared the twins to objects that appear in pairs like two eyes, two hands, two legs of a man or the two wings of a bird.

10. *Sage Ayodha Dhaumya and Uddalaka Aruni*

Once, there lived a sage named Áyodha Dhaumya who had three disciples – Áruni, Upamanyu and Veda. One day, the sage ordered Áruni to stop a breach in the waterway in a certain field. Aruni went there and found that water had breached the field and was moving away from its designated path. Aruni lay down on the breach and prevented the water flow using his body. He stayed there all night. Later in the morning, the sage along with the other disciples came to the spot. There, he saw Aruni lying cold and wet. Seeing the dedication and sincerity of Aruni, the sage was very pleased with Aruni and gave him the title Uddalaka (The one who was raised from the boundary). Later, Aruni became a very famous sage under the name of Uddalaka Aruni.

11. *Harishchandra, the Epitome of Truth*

In ancient times, there was a king named Harishchandra who was truthful, kind-hearted and honest. Once, he accidentally interrupted a sage's meditation and had to pay a lot of money as a fine. He gave away everything he had but still owed more. To keep his promise, he even sold his wife and son and worked in a cremation ground. He didn't let his wife cremate their dead son because she had no money. But because of his honesty and good heart, even the gods were impressed. They told him that he, his wife, and his son would go to heaven because of their goodness. From then on, Harishchandra's name became a symbol of truthfulness and doing what is right. This story teaches us that being truthful and kind is very important, even in difficult times.

12. *The Upanishads*

Upanishad is a Sanskrit word that is derived from the elements 'upa', 'ni' and 'sad'. Upa means 'near', Ni means 'fixed' and 'sad' means 'to sit'. There are more than 200 Upanishads but traditionally, they are 108 in number. Each Upanishad is a part of one of the Vedas. The Vedas have been divided into four parts: the Samhitas, the Brahmanas, the Aranyakas and the Upanishads. The Samhitas are a collection of hymns. They teach us prayers and blessings. The Aranyakas contain rituals, ceremonies, sacrifices and symbolic sacrifices.

The Aranyakas were developed by the hermits, living in the forests. The Brahmanas are commentaries on the Aranyakas – helping the priests to function in the right way. The Upanishads are dialogues between the Guru and the Shishyas on the mysteries of life. The Brihadaranyaka Upanishad is the oldest of the Upanishads. It was composed in the 1st millennium B.C.E. It is associated with the Yajur Veda.

13. *Invoking Peace*

All the Upanishads began and ended with a Shantipatha or invocation of peace, for averting all evil. Early in the morning, the shishyas would sit at their guru's feet. The sun would shine on the thatched huts of the ashrama. There would be grazing cattle. It would be quiet and still in the forest beyond. Suddenly, it seemed as though wild buffaloes were bounding into the ashrama. Demons could be laughing, disturbing the disciples, pouring blood upon the sacrificial offerings.

These were some threats that the sages faced. So, the guru and the shishyas would begin and end every session by the Shantipatha. They asked Nature and the evil creatures to leave them alone through this prayer. Thus, the Shantipatha was a joint prayer for a specific goal. It was not a general prayer for peace from battles but a precise one for not being disturbed during the study sessions.

14. *Sacrificial Horse*

In ancient Vedic tradition, Asvamedha or sacrificial killing of a horse was one of the four most important rites. In the Asvamedha Yajna, a king who desired power would release an Ashva, or horse, onto the other kings' lands. The kings who accepted his supremacy allowed the horse to move freely in their lands. However, the kings wishing to contest would restrain the horse. There would be a battle.

The king who had let the horse run free would become the ruler of the challenging kings if they were defeated in the battle. Once the horse was back, he was to be Medha or sacrificed in a ceremony organised by the victorious king. Furthermore, the Brihadaranyaka Upanishad states that the sacrificial horse is a symbol of the Atman or human self. Usha, the goddess of dawn, is its head, Surya is its eyes, heaven its belly, the sides are the various directions, and the hooves and legs, the Earth.

15. *The Udgeetha*

Prajapati, the Lord of all who are born, had two types of offspring: the Devas (gods) and the Asuras (demons). They struggled with each other for the mastery of the three worlds. The gods said, "Well, let us overcome the demons at the sacrifice (jyotishtoma) by means of the Udgeetha (chanting of the OM Mantra)."

They approached the god of Vak or speech to chant for them. Vak chanted but he kept the pure and correct pronunciations for himself. The Asuras shot Vak with evil.

Then the gods approached Prana, the god of breathing in through the nose, to chant for them. But he kept the best smells to be drawn in by himself. The demons then pierced him with evil.

The gods then approached Chakshus, the god of eyes and Manas, the god of the mind. Both agreed but suffered sins through their selfishness. Finally, the gods resorted to the god of Ashanya Prana or breathing-through-the-mouth. The demons tried to pierce the god by sin, but they failed. So, by means of the Udgeetha the gods were able to overcome the demons.

16. *The Gift of a Thousand Cows*

Janaka, the king of Mithila, also known as Videha, decided to perform the Vahudakshina-yajna in which many gifts are given away to the assembled Brahmanas. At Janaka's court gathered a multitude of sages, priests, and scholars from various regions of Kuru and Panchala kingdoms. Janaka had a thousand cows put into an enclosure. He tied five gold strips around the horns of each cow. "O honoured Brahmanas, whoever out of you is Brahmistha – the most superior in the subject of Brahm – take these cows away."

Sage Yajnavalkya entered with a disciple named Somashrava. "Walk these cows towards our hermitage," he ordered the disciple. The other sages and scholars assembled in the yajna challenged sage Yajnavalkya. They asked several questions but finally gave up because Yajnavalkya answered them all. Yajnavalkya won the debate and took the cows home.

17. *Yajnavalkya and Maitreyi*

Yajnavalkya had two wives, Maitreyi and Katyayani.

He said to Maitreyi one day, "I am going to renounce this life. Let me divide everything between you and Katyayani."

Katyayani was a down-to-earth woman looking after the household. She accepted her share. Maitreyi too did not try to stop Yajnavalkya but she asked, "O Lord! If indeed the whole earth, full of wealth, belonged to me, would I be immortal through that?" "No," replied Yajnavalkya, "your life would be just like that of people who have plenty. For immortality, however, there is no hope through wealth." "What will I do with that which will not make me immortal? Just let me have your knowledge of Brahm," said Maitreyi. Yajnavalkya then taught her about Brahm, and gave her the most precious of spiritual wealth.

18. *Knowing the Atman*

Yajnavalkya gave Maitreyi his knowledge of Brahm. "People are valuable only because of the Atman within themselves. The Atman is what is to be seen, heard, thought about and meditated upon. The knowledge of Brahm is the means of becoming all." Maitreyi listened keenly.

Yajnavalkya continued, "When a drum is beaten, one cannot distinguish between its particular notes and its general notes. When a conch is blown, one cannot distinguish between its particular notes and its general notes. As the fire from the wet wood gives rise to different types of smoke, similarly the Vedas, the Upanishads, the various accounts and tales of the past are all such emissions. They are like the breath of the Atman." Maitreyi nodded. Yajnavalkya explained, "When a lump of salt is thrown into a bowl of water, it cannot be picked up but wherever one takes a little water from the bowl, it will always taste salty. Similarly, Atman is endless, infinite and pure intelligence."

19. *Shvetaketu*

The son of Aruna, Gautama (also called Uddalaka Aruni), was a wealthy and wise sage who possessed abundance of gold, land, livestock, horses, and servants. He had a young son named Shvetaketu, whom he had taught himself. Shvetaketu went to the assembly-house of Panchala kingdom. At that moment, King Pravahana, who was the son of King Jeevala, arrived there, accompanied by numerous attendants.

Knowing Shvetaketu to be somewhat arrogant, Pravahana greeted him as "Kumara" (son or young fellow).

"I see!" answered Shvetaketu.

"You have received the proper guidance from your father, have you not?"

"Yes!" said Shvetaketu.

"Then you must know how people depart in different ways after death."

"Not that," Shvetaketu said.

"Do you know how they come back to life on the Earth?"

"Not that," answered Shvetaketu. Shvetaketu realised that he had nothing to say, so he went away.

20. *Knowledge of Agni*

Shvetaketu took his grievances to Gautama, his father. "That Pravahana, who addresses himself as a king, questioned me and I was unable to respond." Gautama set out to find the answers from the King. Pravahana remarked, "Those answers are divine gifts; ask for worldly gifts." "My material wealth is abundant. Grant me wealth that is timeless and eternal," uttered Gautama. Gautama proclaimed that he would follow Pravahana as a disciple and remain there. Pravahana was a Kshatriya and thus a king, while Gautama was a Brahmana and thus a sage. But Gautama acknowledged Pravahana as his Guru because he was so eager to learn from him.

Pravahana taught Gautama what he knew. He said, "In a flash of light, Agni or Fire in various forms descends upon deserving men and takes them to Brahmaloka, the abode of Brahma, to dwell there eternally." Gautama was happy to gain knowledge from the King.

21. *Janashruti and Raikva*

Long ago, there lived a King called Janashruti. He was generous. Once, King Janashruti was lying down for some cool air. Two swans flew by. One of them said that King Janashruti's aura was not greater than that of Raikva, the cart-puller. The King sent his servant to find Raikva. The King made several offers to entice Raikva to make him his disciple. But the King was unsuccessful. Finally, he appeared before Raikva as a simple man. Raikva then taught Janashruti, "In this creation, there are many elements which are worshipped as gods. There is the wind that sweeps everything. And among Devas, worshipping the Vayu (wind) and the Prana (the vital breath) is advisable. But all these are moved by the Spirit within. This Spirit is not created by anyone. It exists by itself. And yet, it creates and sustains the Universe. Therefore, having pride, ego and vanity from our little actions takes us away from this truth." The King learnt his lesson.

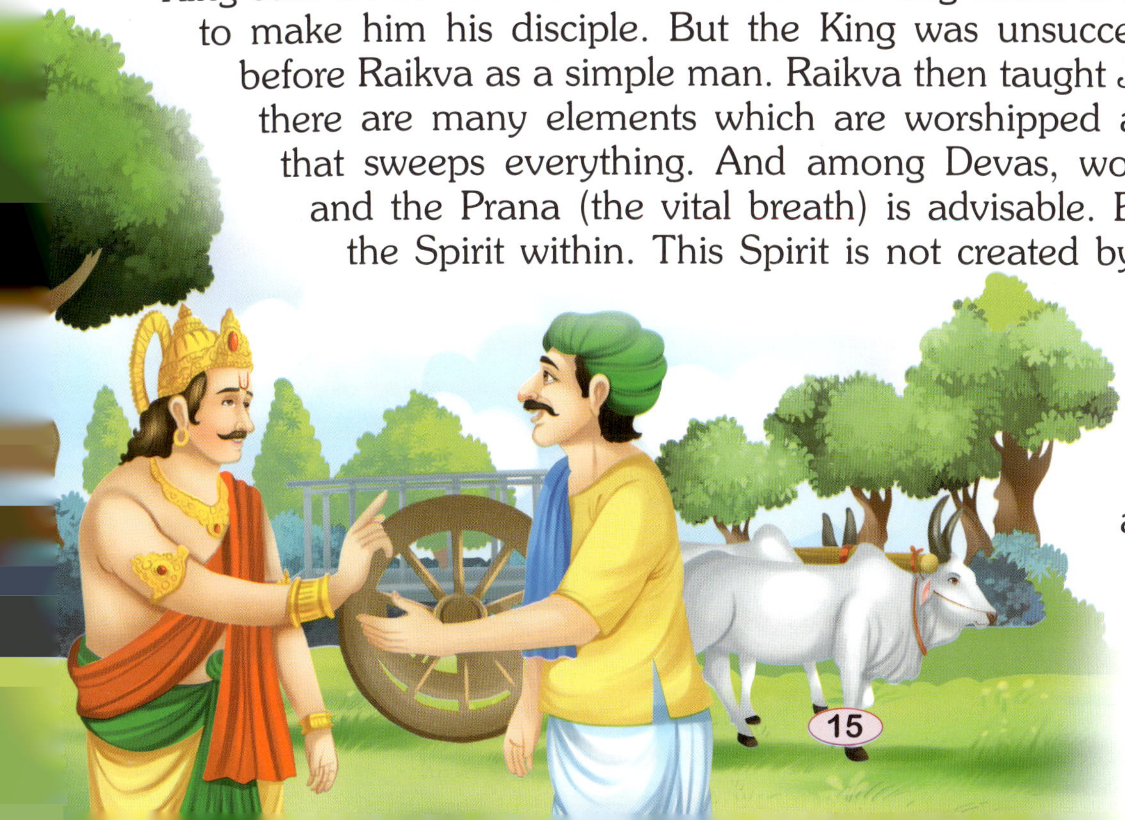

22. *Shvetaketu's Arrogance*

Shvetaketu was the only son of Sage Uddalaka Aruni. When he turned twelve, he was asked by his father to go and get his education from a Gurukul. When Shvetaketu returned from the Gurukul after finishing his twelve years' rigorous training in all the branches of knowledge, his father Uddalaka found arrogance in his expression.

His father observed this and asked, "I see that you are thinking yourself to be a great Vedic scholar. My child, have you ever sought out the knowledge of that by which the unheard can be heard, the unseen can be seen, the unknowable can be known?" Shvetaketu was shocked. He had no idea about what his father had asked. So, he requested his father to give him such kind of knowledge.

23. *Shvetaketu Understands 'Being'*

Uddalaka Aruni started, "In the beginning, there was only one Being, and that Being thought, 'I want to be many, so I will create.' Out of this creation came the cosmos. There is nothing in the cosmos that doesn't come from that one Being. Of everything that exists, this Being is the innermost Self."

Shvetaketu asked, "Please teach me more about the Self, Father."

"Let's start with sleep. What happens when we sleep? When a person is absorbed in sleep, he is one with the Self although he doesn't know it. We say he sleeps but we mean he sleeps in the Self. A tethered bird grows tired from flying in every direction, finding no rest anywhere, and settles down at last on the very same perch on which it is tied. In the same way, the mind, tired of wandering around here and there, settles down at last in the Self, its life and breath, to which it is bound. All creatures have their source in that Being."

24. *Shvetaketu Learns 'Tat Tvam Asi'*

"Where can the root of the body be?" asked Shvetaketu. "Where can it be other than in food?" answered Uddalaka, "Food is the root and the body the offshoot. Similarly, try to see water as the root and food the offshoot. Again, try to see energy as the root and water the offshoot – try to know the tree with its root. All this creation emerges from the One and Only Existent Entity Sat, rests in the Sat and merges into the Sat." "What happens when one dies?" "When someone is dying, his Vak merges into Manas, Manas merges into Prana, Prana merges into Tejas, and Tejas merges into that Supreme Divinity. O Shvetaketu, that is what you are–Tat Tvam Asi (You are That)."

But Shvetaketu was not clear about it and asked Uddalaka Aruni to explain it to him again. If it was like this, why weren't the individual entities aware of it?

25. *One Entity*

Uddalaka Aruni explained with an example. "Shvetaketu, bees make honey by gathering nectar from many flowers, so no one drop of honey can say that it came exactly from one specific flower. You can't identify the juice of one particular flower in the honey. And so it is with creatures like us who merge in that Being, whether in sleep or death.

"And as the rivers that flow from the east to the west merge into the sea and become one with it, forgetting that they were ever separate rivers, so all creatures lose their separateness when they merge into the Pure Being.

"That is how we lose awareness of our separate identities once we have merged into the One Entity. And Shvetaketu, that One Entity, that is what you are."

26. *The Life-Force within Us*

"Come with me," invited Uddalaka Aruni. He pointed to a big tree and said, "If you strike at the root of this tree with an axe, what will happen?"

"The tree will give out its sap."

"Does it live or die?"

"It lives on."

"If you strike at the top, it exudes a juice called sap but still lives on. If you strike at the trunk, it exudes its sap but still lives on."

"Yes!" said Shvetaketu.

If from one branch of this tree the life leaves then the branch dries up. If from a second branch it leaves then the branch, too, dries up. If from the whole tree the life leaves then the whole tree dries up."

"That is true!" nodded Shvetaketu.

"You and I are all alive because of this life-force within us."

27. *The Dissolved Salt*

Shvetaketu asked, "Won't you please explain it further to me?" On Shvetaketu's request, Uddalaka Aruni went on with his lessons in terms of questions and answers.

"Put this lump of salt in water, and bring it back tomorrow morning."

Shvetaketu put the salt in a bowl of water and went to sleep. He brought the bowl to his father the next morning. "Now, Shvetaketu, last night the salt which you put into the water, please bring it."

Shvetaketu could not bring it back. Although the grains of salt were there in the water, he could not find them. They had dissolved. "Son, the salt was there in the water but you could not see it. It is thus that the Sat or Brahm is there within us although we cannot see Him."

28. *Sense of Direction*

Shvetaketu asked his father Uddalaka Aruni to go on and so he did.

A man from Gandhara province was taken to a forest and abandoned there blindfolded. Whether he was facing the north or the east or the south or the west, he would shout for help– I have been brought here blindfolded and abandoned. The Sage further explained, "Now imagine that some good man might take off the blindfold and instruct him - Gandhara region is in this direction; kindly proceed along this direction – village to village, by enquiry, instructions and judgement. Ultimately, the man returns to Gandhara region. A man with a Guru is like that. As soon as he is free of his body, he will merge into the Sat." This is how Shvetaketu received knowledge of Brahm from his father.

29. *Prajapati's Disciples*

Once, Prajapati, the creator of the universe, announced, "The Self or Atman is the sinless, ageless and deathless One. It has neither sorrow nor hunger nor thirst. The goal of all its desire is the Truth. It is this Atman that has to be sought after; one should seek to know about it alone. And one who seeks after Atman and knows it, gains possessions of all the three worlds, wins all that is desirable."

Both the gods and the demons heard this announcement and thought, "We must know this Atman or Self and seek this knowledge that promises all the three worlds."

Hence, Indra, the king of the gods, and Virochana, the leader of the demons, approached Prajapati with all the humility of disciples and requested him to impart this knowledge to them. Prajapati accepted them as his disciples and asked them to stay with him for thirty-two years.

30. *Indra and Virochana*

Both Indra and Virochana stayed on living the life of a Brahmachari. At the end of that period, Prajapati called both of them and said, "Go and adorn yourself and look into the pan of water and tell me about your experience." Happy, they went and adorned themselves, looked into the pan of water, came back and replied to Prajapati, "We saw ourselves well dressed and well adorned." "This is Atman, the immortal and fearless, the Brahm," thus confirmed Prajapati.

Both Indra and Virochana went happy and very much satisfied in their hearts. Prajapati saw them going away and exclaimed to himself, 'Whether they are gods or demons, they will inevitably perish if they are satisfied with the mere reflection of the Reality.' Virochana went to the demons and taught them this knowledge by saying that this bodily self is all that we need to know, serve and glorify.

31. *Indra Learns from Prajapati*

Indra realised that something was wrong with what he had learnt about the Atman. He thought, 'As the water reflects a well-adorned body, so does it reflect a blind man if he is blind. How then could the body or its reflection be said to be the deathless Atman?' He turned back. Prajapati asked him to bring firewood for a new initiation ceremony and become a disciple again. This went on again and again. It was at the end of a hundred and one years of being a disciple that Indra learnt from Prajapati what the Atman really is - a bodyless being, beyond happiness and sorrow, life and death.

Indra went back to impart this knowledge to the gods. The gods received the true knowledge and, therefore, live in the full knowledge of their Self. And because Virochana was satisfied with the knowledge of body as self, the demons, even today, live in the ignorance taking body as Self.

32. *Yaksha and Devas*

There was a war between the Devas (gods) and the Asuras (demons). The Devas got victory. They seemed to believe that it was all their glory. They forgot that there was an invisible hand of Brahm behind the victory. So, Brahm decided to show them their place. He appeared before them as Yaksha. Seeing the bright luminous figure, the Devas were intrigued as to who this Yaksha was. So, they deputed Agni to go and find who the Yaksha was.

As Agni approached the Yaksha, the Yaksha asked him who he was. "I am Jataveda or Agni," he introduced himself.

"What powers do you have?"

"I can burn things up," answered Agni.

The Yaksha then placed a small dry blade of grass before Agni and asked him to show his power by burning it. Agni tried with all his might but failed. Agni returned to the Devas and confessed his inability to find out the Yaksha's identity.

33. *The Being Behind Gods' Victory*

Then the Devas deputed Vayu to go and find out who the Yaksha was. Vayu went up and said, "I am the powerful Vayu. All that is there on this Earth, I can lift it all up." The Yaksha placed the same small dry blade of grass before Vayu and asked him to exhibit his power by blowing it off. Vayu tried with all his strength but could not. He then returned to the gods, admitting his failure.

The Devas requested their lord, Indra, to find out who the Yaksha was. Indra agreed and went. But even as he approached the Yaksha, Yaksha disappeared. Indra asked Uma, a golden goddess, who the Yaksha was. Uma explained that it was none other than Brahm, whose blessings alone have earned them their victory. He appeared before them out of compassion to cure them of their vanity.

34. *Two Famous Prayers from the Upanishads*

The Shanti Mantras or Pancha Shanti mantras are Hindu prayers for peace, found in the Upanishads. Generally, they are recited at the beginning of religious rituals and discourses. They are as follows: *Asato ma sadgamaya* (Lead me from untruth to truth), *Tamaso ma jyotirgamaya* (Lead me from darkness to light), *Mrityor ma amritam gamaya*. (Lead me from death to immortality). The following prayer is chanted at the end of many ceremonies. It is as follows:

Madhu vata hritayatey Madhu ksharanti sindhavah Madhvirna santvoshadhih

Madhu naktamutoshaso Madhumat parthivam rajah Madhu dyourasti nah pita. For us, who are the devotees of the Supreme Truth:

May the winds blow sweetly! May the rivers flow sweetly! May the herbs be to us sweet and beneficial! May there be sweetness during the day and during the night! May the particles of the earth be carrying sweetness for ever!

35. *What are Puranas?*

The word 'Puranas' literally means ancient or old. The Puranas are old tales, but not so old as the Vedas or the Upanishads. There are 18 Maha Puranas and 18 Upa Puranas. The first versions of the various Puranas were likely composed between the 3rd and 10th centuries CE.

After composing the Mahabharata, Vedavyasa composed 400,000 shlokas which his disciple heard. They contained thrilling accounts of gods and demons, sky-spirits, water-snakes, strange lands and magic happenings.

The disciple was a wandering minstrel and charioteer. He went from one place to another. He recounted these tales to a variety of audiences he met.

The stories created enjoyment. They made the hearers' hair (Loma or Roma) stand up (Harshana). The story-teller thus came to be called Lomaharshana or Romaharshana.

Lomaharshana told these stories to his disciples. They told them to theirs. Hence, these ancient stories grew widespread. They became the Puranas.

36. *Ganga's Descent on Earth*

Bhagiratha was a legendary king of the Ikshvaku dynasty. He brought the River Ganga to the Earth from the heavens because she alone could bestow nirvana to Bhagiratha's ancestors who were cursed by Sage Kapila. Bhagiratha prayed to Ganga. She finally agreed to come down to the Earth and flow over the ashes of his ancestors. Bhagiratha prayed to Lord Shiva and requested him to hold Ganga in his matted hair or tresses. Lord Shiva agreed.

Ganga came down from the sky at a great speed. She fell upon the head of Lord Shiva at Mount Kailasa and got caught in his hair. Lord Shiva is known as *Gangaadhara* as he absorbed the flow of Ganga. Lord Shiva saw Bhagiratha waiting patiently for Ganga. So, he released Ganga. Ganga touched the ashes and Bhagiratha's ancestors attained eternal rest in heaven.

37. *The Three Godheads*

Once, there ensued a fight between Brahma and Vishnu. Brahma said, "I am superior because I created you." Vishnu said, "You cannot live without me sustaining, so I am superior." Suddenly, there appeared a pillar (linga) of light. It was decided that whoever would find the end of light would be superior. Brahma took the form of a white swan and flew up. Vishnu took the form of a huge white boar and dived down. They could not find the end of the pillar. Brahma caught a ketaki flower falling downwards from the sky and lied that he found it at the head of the pillar. Shiva, who had taken the form of the pillar, appeared before them. At that moment, they heard the deep sound of three syllables—A-U-M—pronounced together as AUM or OM. This expresses the unity of three entities–Brahma the Creator (indicated by 'A'), Vishnu the Preserver (indicated by 'U') and Maheshwara or Shiva the Destroyer (indicated by 'M').

38. *Shiva, the Destroyer*

The sight of such a beautiful form astonished Brahma and Vishnu. They greeted him as Devesha, Mahesha, Maheshwara, Mahadeva, Hara, and Bhava.

"It is a good thing that we got into a fight," said Vishnu, "This being came to stop our fight! Otherwise, we would have never got to see this being!" Shiva asked Brahma to create the Universe and Vishnu to protect it. He said, "I am split into three, namely Brahma, Vishnu and Hara. There will be born another god from my parts – Rudra. He is not different from me. Brahma, Vishnu and Rudra or I myself – are variations of the same One and Only (Ekamevadvitiyam) entity. Brahma-Vishnu-Shiva is the Hindu trinity, also called the Trimurti. The Supreme Spirit or Universal Truth, called Brahm, is represented in three forms, each corresponding to one cosmic function. Brahma is the Creator, Vishnu is the Preserver and Shiva is the Transformer or Destroyer.

39. *Origin of Rudra*

Prakriti, the primal feminine form, also split into three goddesses. They became the wives of the three godheads. Vishnu took Lakshmi, Brahma took Sarasvati, while Shiva himself took Kali to his side.

Shiva instructed Vishnu and Brahma to build images of the Linga with gold, silver, gems or clay. This is the beginning of Lingapuja or the worship of Shiva by means of the Linga.

Brahma first created some Manasaputras or 'Sons of the Mind' and then some Rishis. But the created beings did not want to have sons. They refused to help Brahma take his creation forward. They chose to remain brahmacharis. Brahma became angry. And while he was angry, Rudra emerged from his forehead.

40. *Sati in Daksha's Yajna*

Daksha was one of the Prajapatis. He was the son of Brahma, and among his foremost creations. Sati, Daksha's youngest daughter, was married to Shiva or Rudra. Daksha disagreed to and opposed the marriage.

He decided to divide the world into those who valued his way and those who did not. So, he asked people not to make offerings to Rudra when they were performing Yajnas. He conducted a Yajna himself where he invited everyone, but not Rudra.

Sati was not aware of Daksha's insult to Rudra. She went there without invitation and without Rudra. Rather than being welcomed, Sati was mocked at. Daksha also insulted Sati's husband. Unable to bear her father's cruel words, Sati jumped into the sacrificial pyre. The unmoved Daksha continued with the Yajna as before. The news reached Rudra at Mount Kailasa. He flew into a rage and sent his companions (ganas) to disrupt the ceremony.

41. *Shiva's Rage*

Meanwhile, Rudra angrily pulled out a lock of hair and dashed it against the mountain. It got divided into two parts. From one part manifested the valiant Veerbhadra and from the other part Mahakali. Both Veerbhadra and Mahakali were instructed by Shiva to destroy the Yajna of Daksha and to kill all the people who were present during the time of Sati's death, including the deities and the sages.

Daksha prayed to Vishnu to rescue him from the imminent wrath of Rudra. Suddenly, there was a loud commotion. The army of Veerbhadra had arrived. A terrible battle was fought between the armies of Veerbhadra and the deities. The deities got defeated and fled away. Daksha ran for his life and hid himself behind the altar where the Yajna was being performed. But Veerbhadra pulled him out from there and severed his head. He then threw his head in the agni-kunda. After this, he returned back to Mount Kailasa.

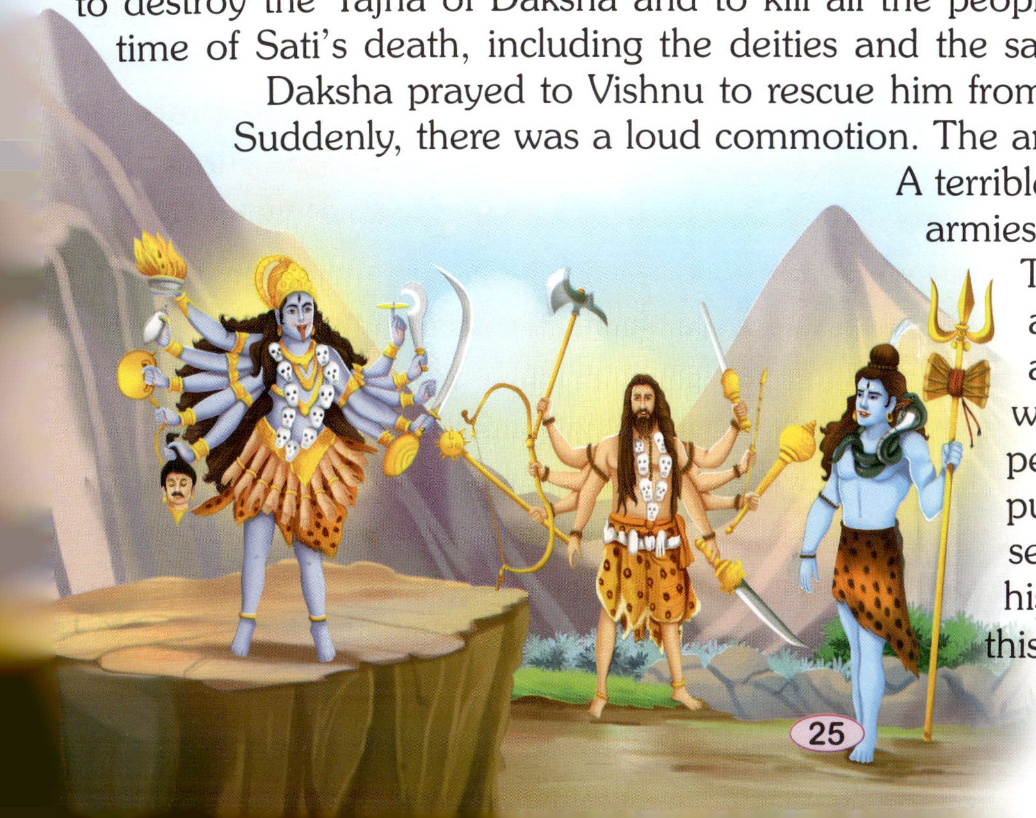

42. *Tarakasura*

After the death of Sati, Shiva went into meditation in the Himalayas and was no longer interested in the world. Taking advantage of the situation, a demon named Taraka pleased Brahma by performing the most rigorous tapasya and got two boons. As the first boon, he asked Brahma to make him the most powerful man in the world. As the second boon, he sought that his death should happen only at the hands of a son born to Shiva. After getting the boons, Tarakasura started attacking the demigods, the saints and the humans. He defeated all the kings and the Devas and took control over the earth and heaven.

All the Devas and the saints sought refuge at the feet of Brahma who told that the only solution to their problem was to bring back Lord Shiva to the world.

43. *Kamadeva is Burnt to Ashes*

Brahma told them that Sati was reborn as Parvati, the daughter of Himalaya. As she often called out "U-Ma" to her mother, she was also called Uma. Parvati also wanted Shiva as her husband. Brahma asked the gods to take the help of Madan or Kamadeva, the god of love.

Indra called Madan, also called Kandarpa. Madan carried a bow of flowers from which he shot arrows into hearts and created love. He came with his wife Rati or Love-play, and his friend Vasanta, or Spring.

They turned the cave that Shiva meditated in, into a garden of pleasure, filled with flowers, trees, birds and bees. Madan shot Shiva with the arrows of desire. The arrows had no effect on Shiva. He was, however, angry at being disturbed. Enraged, Shiva opened his third eye and burned Kamadeva to ashes.

44. *Parvati Prays for Shiva*

Parvati was determined to make Shiva her husband. She gave up all worldly pleasures and underwent penance in the forests. Her tapasya was intense and she survived on nothing but a leaf per day, which too she gave up after a while. Shiva finally decided to test her devotion one last time. He took the form of a human Brahmin and met Parvati. Parvati greeted him with respect but was shocked when the man started speaking ill of Shiva. He said that she was being very silly in praying so hard for Shiva. Parvati was enraged and asked him to leave at once. Shiva assumed his true form and granted Parvati her wish to marry him. Overjoyed, Parvati said that she was none other than Sati, the wife he had been mourning for so long.

45. *What is Avatara?*

The word 'Avatara' is the incarnation of a deity in human or animal form to counteract an evil and protect the world.

Among Brahma, Vishnu and Maheshwara, it is Vishnu, the Preserver who has appeared in various Avataras. The term usually refers to the 10 avataras of Vishnu: Matsya (Fish), Kurma (Tortoise), Varaha (Boar), Narasimha (Half lion and Half-man), Vamana (Dwarf), Parashurama (Warrior with an Axe), Rama (Prince of Ayodhya), Balarama (the elder brother of Krishna), Krishna (Philosopher and Guide) and Kalki (the mighty warrior saviour yet to come).

Kalki is yet to make the tenth Avatara. While his incarnations might have been different, they all stood for the values of Dharma and righteousness and ensured that good always prevails over evil.

46. *Kurmavatara (Vishnu's Incarnation as a Tortoise)*

Kurmavatara was the second incarnation of Lord Vishnu in the form of a tortoise (kurma), who helped the gods and the demons to churn the ocean.

Long ago, the gods and the demons were advised to do Samudra Manthan (churning the ocean) for Amrita. They were told that Amrita would keep them from being dead. As the ocean was deep, they wondered how to churn it. They needed a rod and a rope and a platform on which the rod would move. Hence, Mount Mandar was selected as a rod, Vasuki (big serpent) as a rope and Lord Vishnu transformed himself into a big tortoise (Kurma), the back of whom, would serve as a platform for Mount Mandar. Many wonderful things had come out of the ocean before the gods could get Amrita. The Kurma Purana is believed to be dated around AD 900, wherein Lord Vishnu in the form of a kurma explains the purpose of life.

47. *Durvasa Curses Indra*

What was the need for Samudra Manthan? It is narrated in the Vishnu Purana.

Durvasa was the son of Sage Atri. Once, while wandering, he went to a charming forest. There, a nymph stood with a garland of Parijat flowers in her hand. That garland was made of divine flowers. The divine smell of flower was making the entire forest province fragrant. Durvasa asked the nymph to give him that beautiful garland. The nymph bowed respectfully and gave him the garland.

Durvasa went to Indraloka to see Indra. At that time, Indra was planning to go out somewhere. Durvasa presented the garland of Parijat flowers to Indra. Indra, after receiving the garland from Durvasa, kept it carelessly on the forehead of his elephant-Airavat. The elephant trampled the garland under its feet. This infuriated Durvasa. He cursed Indra, "Lakshmi, the goddess of prosperity, who resides in these flowers, will now desert you."

48. *Vishnu's Plan*

Durvasa's words came to be true and Indra found that not only heaven but also the three worlds had become bereft of goddess Lakshmi. Prosperity vanished and poverty prevailed everywhere. The deities went to take the help of Brahma. Brahma took the deities to Vishnu.

Vishnu told them to do Samudra Manthan to take out Amrita but he also told them that this was not possible without the help of the demons. So, he advised them to take their help. Indra then met Bali and they agreed on doing Samudra Manthan together and also agreed to distribute Amrit between themselves equally. Vishnu said, "I will take incarnation as Kurma. If the ocean was churned with the help of Mount Mandar and Vasuki then goddess Lakshmi would manifest herself. I would hold the mountain on my back." This way, the churning of the ocean commenced.

49. *Churning of the Ocean*

Vasuki wound himself around Mount Mandar. To do Samudra Manthan, the gods had to pull Vasuki from the one side and the demons to pull Vasuki from the other side. The demons refused to grab the tail of Vasuki as they considered it insulting. So, the gods started pulling Vasuki from the tail side and the demons from the head side. As the churning began, big fire flares started coming out of Vasuki's mouth and the demons repented their decision.

The first thing, which came out of the mighty ocean, was the poison Kalkut. Shiva drank it but did not allow it to enter his stomach. He accumulated it in his throat. So, his throat turned blue. Therefore, Shiva is also known as 'Neelkanth'.

The churning continued. The ocean yielded wonderful beings and objects– Surabhi, the cow, Varuni, the goddess of intoxicating drinks and the fragrant flower Parijata.

50. *Lakshmi Emerges*

Next to come was Dhanvantari, dressed all in white with the pot of Amrita in his hands. At the sight of the Amrita, the gods, the demons and the sages were delighted. But there was more to come. There emerged a lotus flower with the shining form of goddess Lakshmi. She held another lotus in her hand.

The sages began to chant hymns in praise of her. The gandharvas sang and the apsaras danced. Rivers like Ganga arrived so that Lakshmi could have a bath. There were eight elephants which protected the eight directions. These elephants took clear water from golden vessels and bathed the goddess. The ocean gave her a garland of lotus flowers which would not fade. Vishvakarma provided the jewels. Thus bathed, dressed, jewelled and garlanded, Lakshmi embraced Vishnu. Since the demons did not like Vishnu, this meant that Lakshmi had forsaken the demons.

51. *Vishnu Tricks Demons*

The demons grabbed the pot of Amrita from Dhanvantari. But Vishnu assumed the form of Mohini to trick the demons of the Amrita and gave it to the gods.

The gods drank the Amrita and attacked the demons with swords. The Amrita had made the gods strong and the demons were no match for them. Their armies scattered and they fled into the netherworld. The gods were delighted. They bowed before Vishnu and continued to rule over heaven. The sun went back to its old path across the sky, so did the stars. Indra ascended his throne and ruled over the three worlds, after having prayed to goddess Lakshmi.

Indra's prayers pleased Lakshmi and she agreed to grant him boons. The first boon was that Lakshmi should never leave the three worlds. And the second boon was that Lakshmi should never turn away from anyone who prays to her using the same prayer that Indra had used.

52. *The Varaha Avatar*

Varaha, the Boar, is the third avatara of Lord Vishnu. Varaha is the symbol of the restoration of the earth and the establishment of a new age. He is depicted as carrying a conch-shell and a discus while holding up the Earth. He is shown standing on the seashore with the serpent Sheshanaga at his feet.

Hiranyaksha was a demon. He was the son of Diti and Kashyapa and the younger brother of Hiranyakashipu. He had received Brahma's blessings and became powerful. Once, he was engaged in war with the gods and took the Earth in the depths of the ocean. Vishnu incarnated into Varaha, a boar, with huge tusks and went down to the ocean. Varaha challenged Hiranyaksha for a battle. The demon ridiculed Varaha who grew in size and lifted the Earth onto his tusks. He slew the demon after a thousand-year-long battle. Afterwards, Varaha rose from the ocean with the Earth in his tusks and placed her gently above it in her original position.

53. *Brahma Gives Boon to Hiranyakashipu*

Hiranyakashipu had always been against Vishnu. He prayed to Brahma standing silently in neck-deep water for a thousand years. Brahma was really pleased with Hiranyakashipu's devotion, and granted him any boon that he wished for. Hiranyakashipu told him that he wanted to be immortal. Brahma told him that such a wish wasn't possible, as it would destroy the order of balance of life. Hiranyakashipu asked Brahma to grant him a boon that would allow no man, god or animal created by Brahma to kill him. Also, nobody could kill him at day or night, and no one could kill him in heaven or on the earth. Also, no one could kill him with a weapon, or kill him either inside or outside his house.

Brahma granted Hiranyakashipu the boon that he asked. The gods, the sky-spirits, and the sages, were all worried at Brahma's granting this boon. Brahma assured them that Vishnu would come down to the Earth and kill Hiranyakashipu.

54. *Prahlad, a True Devotee of Vishnu*

Hiranyakashipu grew over-confident with his boons. He fought with the gods and became the ruler of heaven. However, his own son Prahlad was a great devotee of Lord Vishnu. With the passage of time, Hiranyakashipu got furious at Prahlad for praying to Vishnu. Finally, he asked his guards to kill Prahlad. The guards reluctantly agreed to kill him, but with each blow on Prahlad, their swords crumbled to pieces and Prahlad remained unharmed.

Hiranyakashipu asked for some poisonous snakes to bite Prahlad, but Prahlad still remained unharmed. He then let loose mad elephants at him, but the elephants did not attack him. He decided to call his sister Holika, and ordered her to make him sit on her lap and burn him to his death. He thought that this plan would work at least, but it was Holika, who was immune to fire, who was reduced to ashes.

55. *The Narasimha Avatara*

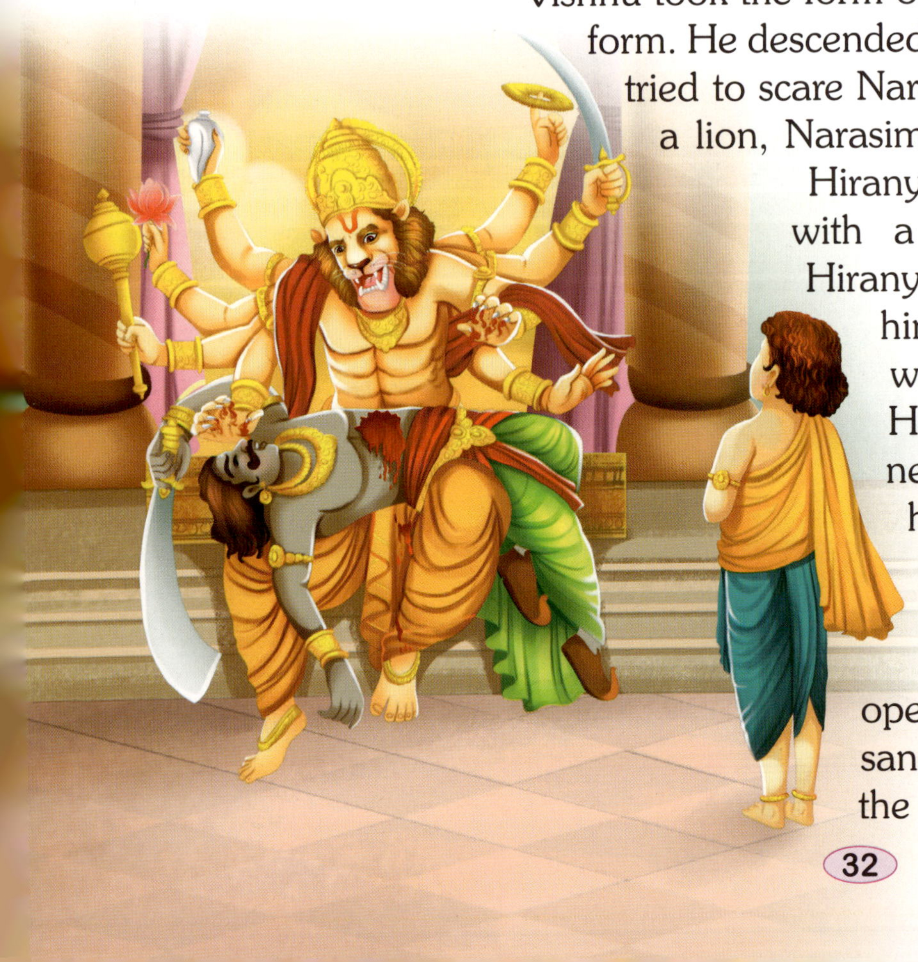

Vishnu took the form of Narasimha, a half-lion and half-human form. He descended to Hiranyakashipu's court. The demons tried to scare Narasimha by shouting at him. Roaring like a lion, Narasimha began to eat them up.

Hiranyakashipu took up a flaming spear, but with a roar Narasimha broke it. He held Hiranyakashipu in a vice–like grip and dragged him to the threshold of the door, which was neither outside nor inside his house. He placed him on his lap, which was neither the sky nor the earth, and killed him with his claws at twilight, without using any weapons. Brahma's boon could not protect Hiranyakashipu. Vishnu in his Narasimha Avatara ripped open his chest with his claws. The gods sang in praise of Vishnu. Prahlad became the king of the land.

56. *The Vamana Avatara*

The Vamana Avatara starts with Mahabali, the demon-king. Mahabali was the grandson of Prahlad and son of Virochana. Bali went to battle against Indra. He won the battle and Indra fled from the battlefield.

Indra underwent penance so as to please Vishnu. Maharshi Kashyap's wife Aditi, who was Indra's mother, saw her son in trouble and went to Vishnu for help. Vishnu said, "I will help you, Devamata. I will be born as your son in the near future. I will then kill Bali."

Very soon, Aditi was blessed with a son. He was very short. She named him Vamana. Meanwhile, Bali had begun a Yajna. Shukra, the Acharya or preceptor of the demons, was conducting it. Vamana posed as a Brahmana reached there. Shukracharya warned Bali, "This Vamana is none other than Vishnu. Whatever he wants, refuse!"

57. *Three Footsteps*

Bali did not pay any heed to the advice from Shukracharya. He asked Vamana, "How can I help you?" Vamana said, "I just need the land that my three steps cover." The Asuras laughed at the request. Bali agreed to grant him what he wanted. Suddenly, Vamana started growing in size. Soon he was larger than planet Earth itself. He took a large step and put it on the Earth to claim it and said, "Now the Earth is mine." Then he took the second step and put it on heaven and said, "Now heaven is mine." Then he said, "Bali, where should I keep my third step? The Earth and heaven are already mine." Bali then addressed Vamana and said, "As nothing else is left, you may keep your third step on my head."

Hearing Bali's words, Vishnu appeared in his true form and said, "I bless you, Bali. From now on, you shall rule Pataal Lok forever."

58. The Parashurama Avatara

Parashurama was born to Rishi Jamadagni and Devi Renuka. Jamadagni was a Brahmin sage and his wife Renuka was a Kshatriya. Jamadagni and Renuka performed penance for several years to appease Shiva so that the sixth incarnation of Lord Vishnu would be born to them. Shiva granted them the boon and Vishnu incarnated as their fifth and youngest child and was named Rambhadra.

One day, Jamadagni was angry with his wife, and ordered his eldest son to kill his mother. He refused. Jamagadni asked the next three sons. They too refused to kill their mother. Jamadagni cursed all of them. When Jamadagni turned to Rama, he beheaded his mother with his axe. Jamadagni was pleased with Rama's righteousness and asked him for the boon. He asked his father to restore the life of his mother and Sage Jamadagni granted his request.

59. Kamadhenu, the Celestial Cow

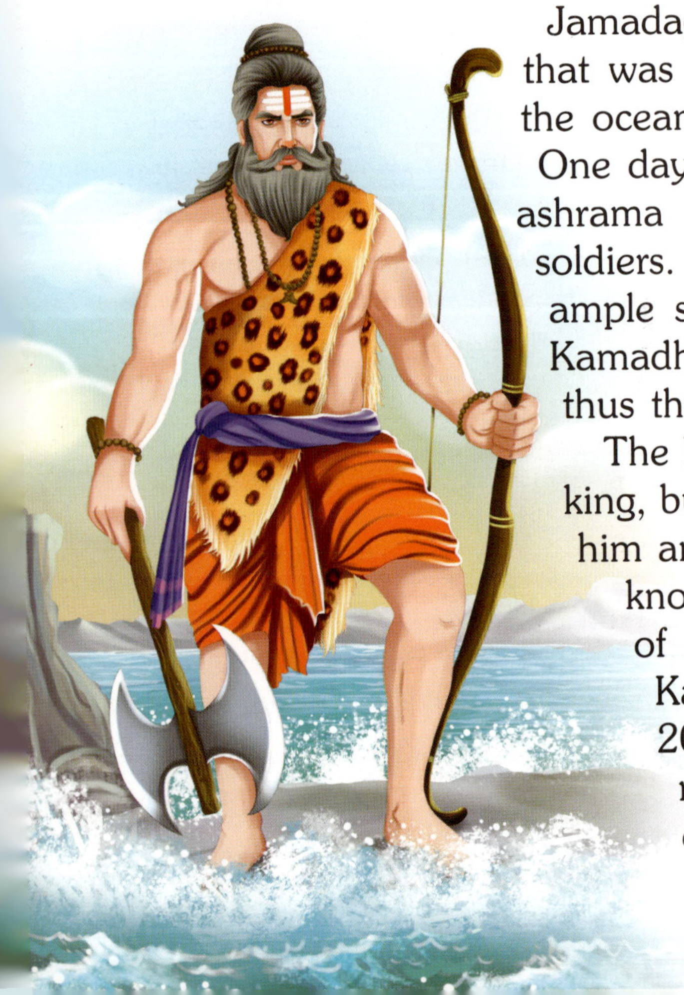

Jamadagni and Renuka had a magical cow called Kamadhenu that was the symbol of abundance. It had emerged out of the ocean during the great churning.

One day, king Kartavirya Arjun with his soldiers visited the ashrama of Jamadagni. Jamadagni provided food to his soldiers. The curious king asked for the secret behind this ample supply. Jamadagni told him about his divine cow, Kamadhenu. It offered him everything the sage needed, and thus there was no shortage of food in the ashrama.

The king asked Jamadagni to give the divine cow to the king, but the sage denied it. As a result, the king beheaded him and abducted the cow. When Rama came, he got to know the injustice. He took an oath to rid the Earth of all the Kshatriyas. He took up his axe and killed Kartavirya Arjun. But he did not stop there. He fought 20 more times to finish all the cruel Kshatriyas and restore Dharma in the Treta Yuga. People began to call him Parashu-Rama (Rama with the Axe).

60. *The Rama Avatara*

A king named Moolagan escaped Parashurama's wrath and thus he was responsible for the continuance of the Kshatriya clan. His descendant Raghu was a king of great valour. He had a son called Aja. Aja's son was Dasharatha. The well-fortified city of Ayodhya was their capital.

The seventh incarnation of Vishnu, Rama, is said to have taken birth on the earth to annihilate the evil forces of the Treta Yuga. Ravana, the demonic ten-headed king of Lanka having pleased Brahma by his austere penance, attained the boon of being invulnerable from the wrath of the gods and now ruled heaven and the earth. Lord Vishnu divided himself into four beings and was born as Dasharatha's four sons, namely Rama, Bharata, Lakshmana and Shatrughna, to his wives Kausalya, Sumitra and Kaikeyi.

61. *The Exile of Rama*

Rama, Lakshmana, Bharata and Shatrughna grew up learning all the arts. Once, sage Viswamitra asked Dasaratha's help in slaying the demons who were disturbing him in his yajnas. Sage Visvamitra asked for Rama and Lakshmana to accompany him to the forest to fight against the demons. Rama and Lakshmana accompanied him to the forest and helped him by slaying Tadaka and all the demons who dared to interfere. The pleased Viswamitra took them to Mithila, where Rama lifted Lord Shiva's Dhanush and married Sita, daughter of King Janaka. Dasharatha, growing old and tired, wanted to give over the rule of Ayodhya to Rama. But because of a plot hatched within the palace, Rama had to leave it for fourteen years. His wife Sita and brother Lakshmana went with him. Dasharatha died of grief. Bharata and Shatrughna took care of Ayodhya while Rama moved through the jungle.

62. *Rama Fights Ravana*

A series of events led to the demon-king Ravana carrying Sita away to his kingdom Lanka beyond the sea. Rama and Lakshmana hunted for Sita everywhere. They gathered together a band of monkeys and bears, who helped them to find her in Lanka.

With the help of the monkeys and the bears, Rama and Lakshmana built a bridge across the sea. After a fierce battle with the demons at Lanka, Rama was able to kill Ravana. He made peace with the rakshasas. Vibheeshana was crowned king of Lanka. Rama thanked all his friends for their valuable help and returned to Ayodhya. Rama was crowned king and he ruled justly for a long time.

Rama, one of the most adulated incarnations of Vishnu, is referred to as Maryada Purushottama or the Perfect Man.

63. *Balarama's Birth*

In the Dwapara Yuga, the evil king Kansa, brother of Devaki, was intent upon killing the children of his sister because of an Akashvani (celestial prediction) that he would die at the hands of her eighth child. Kansa had already killed the first six children of Devaki.

Lord Vishnu incarnated as Balarama when Indra and the other gods came to him for help. Vishnu took one black and one white hair from his head and promised that these two would come to fight against the demons. This way, first Balarama (the white hair) and then Krishna (the black hair) incarnated in the womb of Devaki. Balarama appeared as the seventh child in the womb of Devaki. Vishnu instructed Yogamaya, His internal potency, to transfer the unborn child from the womb of Devaki to that of Rohini, one of the other wives of Vasudeva. In this way, Balarama was born in Gokul under the protection of Nanda Maharaja.

64. *The Krishna Avatara*

Lord Vishnu descended on the Earth as Krishna, the son of Devaki and Vasudeva. In his early years, Krishna killed various demons and tyrant kings. He also became a highly respected advisor of the Pandavas who were a branch of Chandra-vamsha, Puru-vamsha or Kuru-vamsha. They were thrown out of Hastinapura by their cousins– the Kauravas.

Krishna was a great friend of the third Pandava, Arjuna. Krishna's sister Subhadra was married to Arjuna. Krishna tried to bring about peace between the Kauravas and the Pandavas. He went to the court of the Kauravas as a messenger of peace. But Duryodhana, the eldest of the Kauravas, did not agree. He tried to take Krishna prisoner. Then Krishna showed his Vishvaroopa or Universal-form. Duryodhana let him go free. Krishna in his Vishvaroopa is a striking form of the Krishna Avatara.

65. *Krishna in Kurukshetra*

The Kauravas and the Pandavas finally fought a battle on the plains of Kurukshetra. Many kings and princes joined them. Many of them were killed and the Pandavas won the battle. Although Krishna did not fight in the battle, he did drive Arjuna's chariot. Krishna urged Arjuna to continue fighting, but with a detached attitude, when he began to question Arjuna's ability to defeat so many of his own relatives.

The advice is world-famous as the holy Bhagvad Gita. Much later, Krishna's entire clan– the Yadavas– died fighting among themselves. Sad Krishna went and sat under a banyan tree, with his leg outstretched, and he started shaking it. A hunter, who was hunting in the forest, saw the movement through the bush, thought it was a deer, and shot it. An arrow pierced Krishna's heel and he departed to Vishnuloka.

66. *The Buddha and Kalki Avataras*

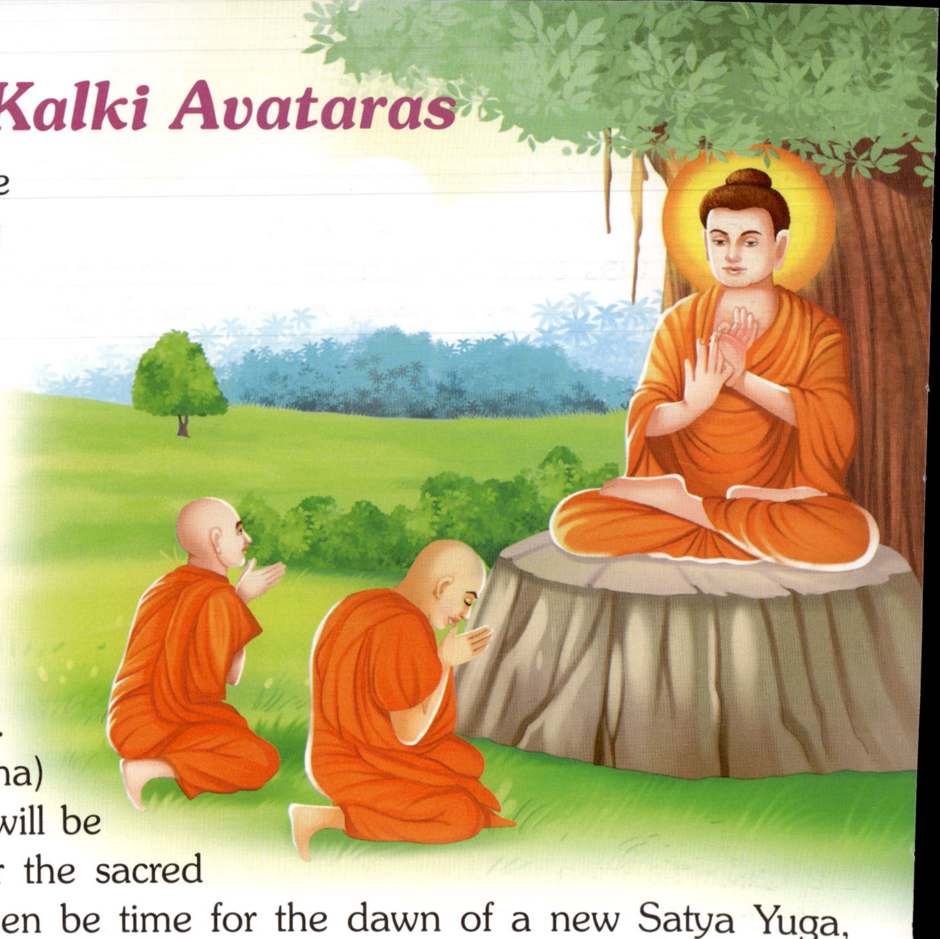

The Buddha Avatara is among the 24 Avataras of Lord Vishnu. According to the Agni Purana, Vishnu was born as Prince Siddhartha of Kapilavastu. He renounced the life of a prince to meditate and become Buddha or the Enlightened One.

The Kalki Avatara is yet to take place in the present era, the Kali Yuga. In this Avatara, Vishnu will take up arms to destroy the disbelievers. Kalki's priest will be sage Yajnavalkya. The norms of the four classes (varna) and the four stages of life (ashrama) will be established again. People will honour the sacred texts and become righteous. It will then be time for the dawn of a new Satya Yuga, a fresh period of righteousness.

67. *Krishna Lifts Mount Govardhan*

Once, when the people of Braj including Nanda Maharaja were planning for the worship of Indra by giving animals in sacrifice, Krishna questioned them as to why they were doing so. Nanda Maharaja explained to Krishna that this was done every year to please Indra. But Krishna debated that they were farmers and they should do only their duty or 'Karma' by concentrating on farming. Finally, convinced by Krishna, the villagers did not perform the worship. Furious with the inhabitants of Braj, Indra decided to punish them by sending terrible rain clouds to flood the land of Vrindavan.

The frightened people approached Krishna for help. Krishna lifted up the entire Mount Govardhan at once with his left hand, and held it up like an umbrella. One by one, all the inhabitants of Vrindavan, along with their cows and other household possessions, took shelter under Mount Govardhan. They were astounded to see the huge Mount Govardhan resting perfectly balanced on Krishna's little finger.

68. *Krishna and Kaliya*

Kaliya, the serpent, was originally from Ramanakadwipa and driven away from there because he was afraid of Garuda, the enemy of snakes. Garuda had been cursed by Sage Saubhari that he would meet his end there if he ever came to Vrindavan. So, Kaliya made Vrindavan his home and lived there with his family.

The giant serpent resided in the river Yamuna and scared people away. None could go where he lived. He also spilled poison into the Yamuna which was frothing and bubbling over. One day, Krishna and his friends were playing a game of ball. While playing, the ball fell near the spot where Kaliya lived. Krishna jumped in after the ball. His friends called out to him, warning him of the dreadful serpent.

Krishna ignored their cries and dived deep into the river to retrieve the ball. Everyone from the village rushed to the river bank, but no one dared to go in after Krishna.

69. *Krishna Dances on Kaliya*

Under water, Kaliya attacked Krishna. He attempted to dig his fangs into Krishna, but Krishna was too fast for him. He filled the water with his venom, but Krishna dispersed the venom with one stroke of his hand. He then wrapped his body around Krishna and dragged him deeper into the river, attempting to crush him. But Krishna grew his body so huge that Kaliya had to release him.

Soon Kaliya started to tire. Krishna then grabbed his tail and dragged him to the river surface. He then assumed the weight of the whole universe in his feet. And playing his flute with one hand, he started dancing on Kaliya's head. Kaliya started to die and began vomiting blood. Kaliya's wives came and begged Krishna to spare his life. Kaliya too surrendered and promised not to trouble anybody again. Krishna forgave him and told him to go back to Ramanakadwipa along with his family, and never come back to Vrindavan again.

70. *Nalakuvara and Manigriva*

In the Bhagavata Purana, Nalakuvara and his brother Manigriva are cursed by sage Narada and turned into trees. They are later released by Krishna.

Nalakuvara and Manigriva were playing naked with the Apsaras in the Ganges when Sage Narada passed by. On seeing Narada, the maidens covered themselves, but Nalakuvara and Manigriva did not notice Narada. Narada cursed them to become two Martu trees.

Many years later, when Krishna was an infant, his mother Yashoda tied him to a mortar to prevent him from eating soil. Krishna dragged the mortar along the ground until it got stuck between two trees. These trees happened to be Nalakuvara and Manigriva and upon contact they returned to their original forms. The brothers then paid homage to Krishna, apologized for their previous wrongs and departed.

71. *Krishna and Sandipani Muni*

According to the Bhagavata Purana, during their stay in the ashrama of Sandipani Muni, Krishna and Balarama acquired complete knowledge and skill in every subject. They asked their teacher for the dakshina (fee). Sandipani Muni asked Krishna to save his child who had vanished in the ocean at Prabhasa. Both the brothers went to Prabhasa and found that the son had been stolen by Panchajana (a demon) who lived in water in the form of a conch. Krishna immediately dived into the sea and found and destroyed the demon, but there was no boy in the demon's stomach. Then he went with Balarama to the abode of Yama, Death. There, he loudly blew the Panchajanya conch and asked Yama to return the boy. The king of Death immediately agreed. Krishna and Balarama then brought their guru's son back home.

72. *Krishna and Sudama*

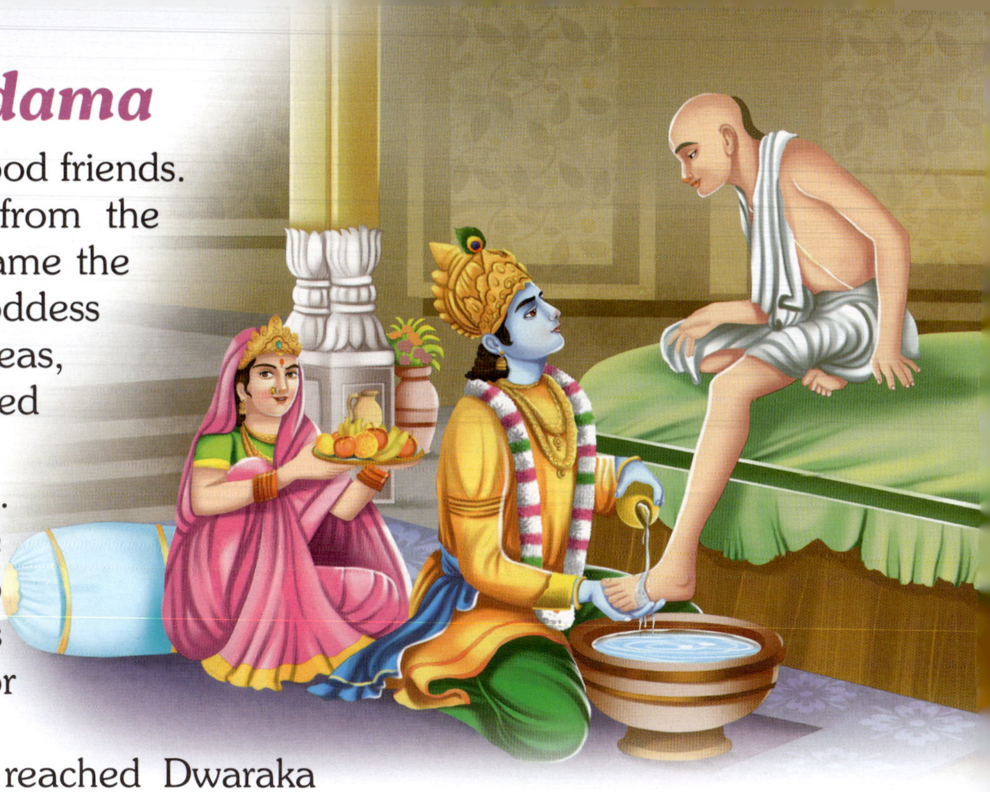

Krishna and Sudama were childhood friends. Both of them gained knowledge from the same guru. Years later, Krishna became the king of Dwaraka and married the goddess of prosperity, Rukmini. Whereas, Sudama became a pandit and married a girl arranged by his parents.

Sudama didn't earn much. Sudama's wife suggested that he should meet Krishna who might help him. On the day of his journey, his wife packed some flattened rice or poha for Krishna.

After days of walking, Sudama reached Dwaraka where he was awed by its prosperity. Seeing his childhood friend, Krishna rushed towards Sudama and hugged him with joy. Krishna and his wife Rukmini then made him sit on a royal seat and washed his feet as a warm gesture. They also served Sudama with delicious dishes. Krishna and Sudama recalled their early childhood days.

73. *True Friendship*

Sudama did not burden Krishna with the stories of his penury, and even felt a little embarrassed about giving Krishna the flattened rice that his wife had packed. However, Krishna had taken notice and playfully snatched it away from him. On opening it, Krishna was delighted to see his favourite snack hidden inside and took a handful of it into his mouth.

The next morning, Sudama took Krishna's leave. However, when he reached his house, he found a grand mansion there instead of his humble hut. His children came running towards him wearing expensive clothes and jewels and his wife was decked out like a queen. She explained to her confused husband that their life got transformed the moment he reached Dwaraka. She later asked him what he asked Krishna. Sudama smiled, "I didn't ask Krishna for anything. He knows it all."

74. *Akrura's Mystic Vision of Krishna*

Kansa knew that Krishna was in Vrindavan and sent many demons to kill him. But Krishna had killed all of them. As Krishna grew, Kansa sent the nobleman Akrura to trick him into coming to Mathura for a tournament. Akrura was a devotee of Lord Vishnu. Although Akrura warned Krishna of the trick, Krishna decided it was time to confront Kansa.

Krishna, Balarama, several gopas (cowherders), and Akrura stopped along the road to Mathura. Akrura asked the brothers to rest in the chariot while he performed a ritual bath in the river. Each time Akrura immersed himself, he experienced a mystic vision of Krishna and Balarama. First, he saw the divine brothers sitting together underwater, although he knew they were actually seated in the chariot on the bank. In his final vision, he perceived their eternal forms–four-armed Vishnu (Krishna) resting on Adishesha, the endless serpent (Balarama).

75. *Fight with Jarasandha*

The father-in-law of Kansa was Jarasandha, the king of Magadha. When Jarasandha heard about Kansa's death, he was furious, and was determined to put an end to the Yadu race. With twenty-three battalions of soldiers, he came to Mathura and laid siege to the city. But Krishna resolved in his mind, 'Those who are helping Jarasandha should be killed first. For, I have come to relieve the earth of her burden. Hence, I will not kill the king of Magadha now.'

Balarama and Krishna put on their armours, got into the chariots, and entered the field of battle with a small army. A fierce battle ensued. At the onslaught of Krishna's arrows and Balarama's plough-weapon, Jarasandha's men began to die. Finally, only Jarasandha remained alive. Grabbing hold of him, Balarama tied him up with a rope and was about to kill him, but Krishna advised Balarama to let Jarasandha go. Humiliated, Jarasandha went back to his own kingdom.

76. *Muchukunda's Boon*

Once in a battle, the devas were defeated by the asuras. They asked King Muchukunda for help and he agreed to help them. Since the devas did not have an able commander, King Muchukunda protected them for a long time. So, when the devas got an able commander like Karttikeya, the son of Shiva, the devas said to the King, "O King! You helped us so much by sacrificing your kingdom and family life. We can offer you one boon except moksha."

Muchukunda said, "I am very tired. I need a long, undisturbed sleep." The devas then said, 'If anybody awakens you while you are sleeping, he shall be burnt to ashes as soon as you look at him." So, Muchukunda entered the cave and fell asleep. Later, Kalayavan was burnt up by the power of the boon.

77. *Kalyavan's Death*

Kalayavan was undefeated and unmatched in battle. Kalayavan joined Jarasandha against Krishna with thirty-five million soldiers. It was feared that Jarasandha and Kalayavan would attack Mathura from opposite sides. Krishna and Balarama decided to build a huge fort far to the west of Mathura. Krishna named it Dwaraka.

Krishna took the Yadus to the new city. Leaving them there, he returned to Mathura with Balarama. While Balarama remained inside Mathura to guard it, Krishna went out alone and unarmed through the main gate. Seeing Krishna unarmed and on foot, Kalayavan threw down his arms and ran after him. Krishna ran up a mountain and went into a cave. In the dark cave, Kalayavan lost sight of him. Then he noticed someone lying down and thought it was Krishna. This was King Muchukunda. He awoke from his slumber in a fury. Looking at Kalayavan, fire came out of his eyes, and Kalayavan was burnt to ashes.

78. *The Syamantaka Jewel*

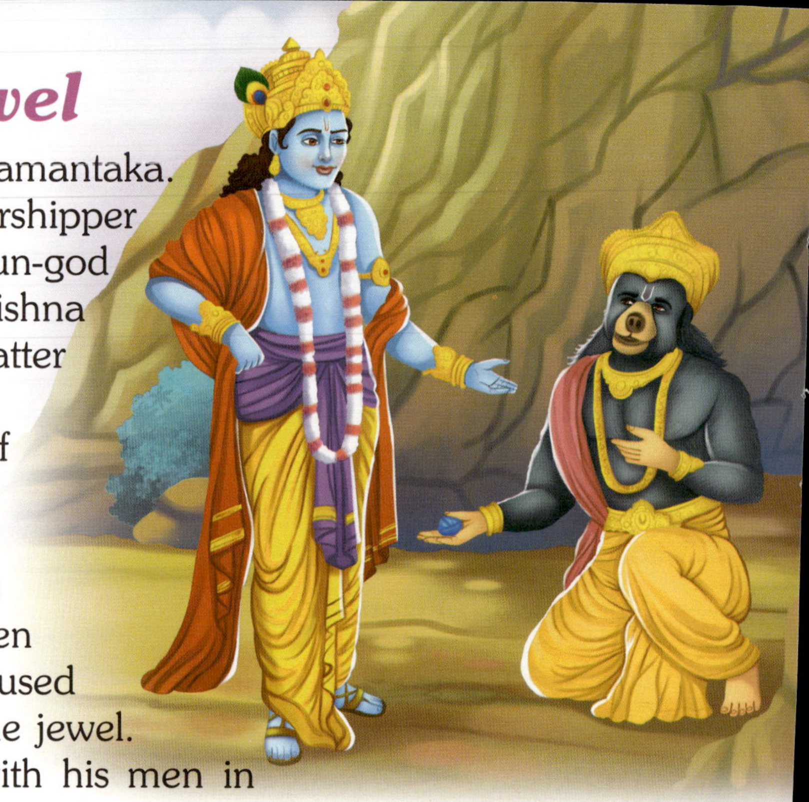

The Sun-god possessed a jewel called Syamantaka. Satrajit, Yadava King, was a devout worshipper of the Sun-god. Pleased with him, the Sun-god gave him this unique jewel. One day, Krishna asked King Satrajit for the jewel but the latter refused his request.

Shortly thereafter, Prasena, the brother of Satrajit, went out hunting wearing the jewel but was killed by a lion. The king of the bears, Jambavan, killed the lion and gave the jewel to his daughter Jambavati. When Prasena did not return, Satrajit falsely accused Krishna of killing Prasena for the sake of the jewel.

To remove all doubts, Krishna set out with his men in search of the jewel and found it in Jambavan's cave, with his daughter. Jambavan attacked Krishna thinking him to be an intruder who had come to take away the jewel. Jambavan and Krishna fought each other for 28 days. In the end, Jambavan finally recognised him as the incarnation of Lord Vishnu and surrendered.

79. *Jambavati and Satyabhama*

Having repented his act, Jambavan gave Krishna the jewel and also his daughter Jambavati in marriage. Now, Krishna came back with the Syamantaka jewel and Jambavati, and he narrated the detailed story of the retrieval of the jewel. Then he returned the jewel to Satrajit in the presence of the citizens of Dwaraka. Satrajit had spread a false allegation against Krishna, so he was utterly ashamed. He pondered over the whole matter and finally decided that he should give the jewel to Krishna. Added to it, he would give away his beautiful daughter Satyabhama. Accordingly, Satrajit handed over to Krishna the jewel along with Satyabhama. Through the usual rituals, the wedding of Satyabhama with Krishna was solemnised. Krishna then addressed Satrajit and said, "You are a worshipper of the Sun-god. The jewel given by him may remain with you. We shall only reap its benefits."

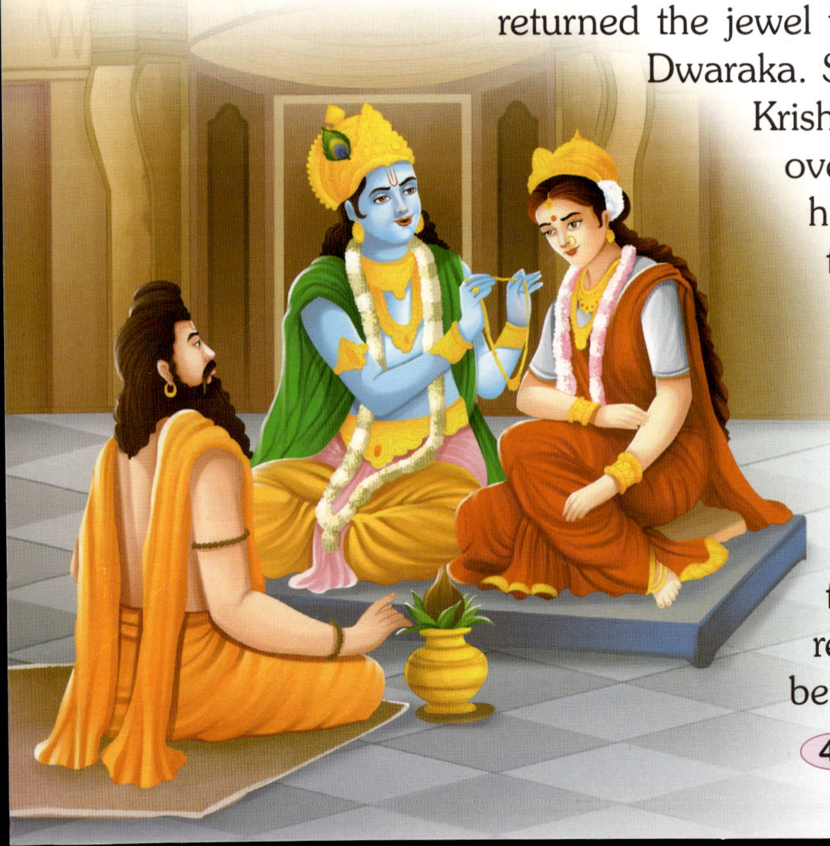

80. *Akshaya Patra*

Akshaya Patra was a divine vessel that was given to Draupadi, by the Sun-god. When the Pandavas and their wife, Draupadi, started their exile, they were worried about how they were going to provide food for the sages that accompanied them into the forest. Sage Dhaumya suggested that Yudhishthira should pray to Surya, as he was the provider of food for all creatures. Upon the sage's advice, Yudhishthira stood in the waters of the Ganga, facing the sun, and prayed to the Surya, eating nothing for several days. He prayed that Surya should bestow food upon them all.

Pleased by his devotion, Surya appeared before him. He gave Yudhishthira the Akshaya Patra– a copper plate that would remain full of food until Draupadi ate. Surya also blessed Yudhishthira and declared that his kingdom would be restored to him at the end of the fourteenth year.

81. *Nara-Narayana*

Nara and Narayana were twin sages who were the incarnated Avataras of Lord Vishnu. Nara means 'human', and Narayana refers to the 'Supreme Lord'. The purpose of their incarnation was to maintain Dharma on the earth. They were widely known as Krishna and Arjuna respectively in the Mahabharata. The Bhagavata Purana mentions Nara-Narayana as the fourth incarnation of Lord Vishnu on the earth.

Nara and Narayana were sons of Dharma (son of Brahma) and Murti (daughter of Daksha). They lived at Badrika performing severe austerities and meditation for the welfare of the world. The sages defeated a demon called Sahasrakavacha (one with a thousand armours). To test them, even Lord Shiva threw his most destructive divine weapon, Pashupatastra, at them. However, the weapon lost its power as it reached near them because of their intense penance and devotion. Shiva realised that they were at the highest level of Samadhi.

82. *Urvashi's Birth*

Urvashi was a heavenly nymph well-known as the most beautiful apsara with excellent dancing skills. The Bhagavata Purana describes the story of her birth.

Once, Nara and Narayana were performing austerity in Badrinath. Their energy was so intense that it scared Indra. So, to interrupt the twin sages from their penance, Indra sent Kamadeva (the god of love and lust) and the Apsaras.

The Apsaras tried their best efforts to disturb Nara and Narayana but failed. Instead, Narayana placed a flower on his thigh from which a beautiful apsara emerged. Her beauty and charm made even the heavenly Apsaras and Kamadeva return to heaven. Since the Apsara originated from the thigh (Uru) of Sage Narayana, she was named Urvashi. Knowing the intention of Kamadeva, Basanta (spring), and the Apsaras, Nara and Narayana were not angry with them. Instead, they requested to take Urvashi with them to heaven.

83. *Krishna and Jarasandha*

Once, Yudhishthira decided to perform the Rajasuya sacrifice. Krishna suggested that it was necessary for them to kill Jarasandha and release the kings under his control for the successful completion of the Rajasuya.

Bhima, Arjuna and Krishna left for Magadha, disguised as Brahmins. When they reached Jarasandha's court, the king declared that he would give the Brahmins whatever they asked for. Immediately, Krishna asked him to combat Bhima. He and Bhima fought fiercely with each other in a duel for the next 27 days. Krishna knew the secret of Jarasandha's birth and, therefore, the key to his defeat. Before the duel, on the 28th day, Krishna picked up a twig, split it into two parts in front of Bhima and threw them in opposite directions. During the duel, Bhima seized Jarasandha by the leg and threw him to the ground. He then tore the body of the king into two halves and threw them away in opposite directions to bring an end to the mighty Jarasandha.

84. *Hayagreeva Avatara*

Hayagreeva, Hayavadana or Hayasirsa was an incarnation of Vishnu with the neck and head of a white horse. He sits on a lotus and symbolises enlightenment. He has four hands, one granting knowledge, the second holding books, the third holding a conch shell and the fourth a bladed discus.

Goddess Shakti (Mother Goddess) blessed Lord Brahma with the Vedas. Brahma was supposed to create the Universe by looking into the Vedas as standard texts. Brahma created two demons, Madhu and Kaitabha, from two water droplets. Unfortunately, Madhu and Kaitabha had stolen the Vedas from Brahma. Without the Vedas, Brahma was not able to perform his duties. He went to goddess Shakti and prayed to her. She suggested him to worship Vishnu to recover the Vedas. Brahma prayed to Vishnu who incarnated as Hayagreeva. He got rid of the demons Madhu and Kaitabha and thus recovered the Vedas. Thus, Hayagreeva became the protector of the Vedas.

85. *Brahma's Fifth Head*

In the Brahma Purana, it is mentioned that once a fierce battle broke out between the Asuras and the Devas. While Brahma stood amidst the armies of the Devas, his fifth head which was of a donkey, brayed loudly, "O Asuras, why do you run away? Why are you scared of the Devas? I shall devour all the Devas for you in a moment." Hearing this, the other gods got scared and approached Vishnu. He heard them out and then said, "If you cut off the head of Brahma and if it falls on the earth, it would destroy the whole Earth. You need a god who could hold his head in hand. Shiva alone has the strength to fulfil such an act." The gods thus approached Shiva who promptly cut off Brahma's fifth head. But the severed head got stuck on his palm and Shiva could not shake it off.

86. *The Sin of Brahmahatya*

Brahma created a fully armed warrior who started chasing Shiva.

Shiva used his Trishul, or trident, to pierce his left hand. Blood spurted out and reached Shiva's forehead. An armoured archer was born and began to fight the warrior that Brahma had sent after Shiva.

After a long fight, Brahma's warrior won over Shiva's. Shiva was still stuck with Brahma's head. It had turned into a skull. Shiva thus roamed the earth as Kapalika, or the skull-bearer.

Suddenly, there appeared a woman, huge, dark and red-haired, who said, "In chopping off the head of Brahma, you have committed the great sin of Brahmahatya. I am that sin, in the shape of a woman." And she went right into Shiva! Shiva sprinted about, shaking off the sin and the skull.

87. *Vishnu Advises Shiva*

Shiva had committed a grave sin of Brahmahatya. All his efforts of separating Brahma's skull from his left palm went in vain. He finally met Vishnu and sought his help. "Go to Varanasi and bathe at the embankment called Dashashvamedha-ghata," said Vishnu.

Shiva rushed there and bathed in the Ganga. The dark woman with red hair had cleared out of him. But the skull still was stuck to his left palm. Shiva once again appealed to Vishnu. Vishnu told him that his problem would be solved if he took a bath in the lake, which was near the temple. Shiva took a bath in that lake and ultimately, the skull fell on the ground. The place where the skull had fallen later on became famous as Kapaalmochan. This way, Shiva became famous as Kapaali.

88. *Garuda and Maninaga*

Anatanaga had a son named Maninaga. Garuda was the enemy of snakes. Maninaga began to pray to Shiva. Having pleased Shiva, he obtained the boon that Garuda would be able to do him no harm. Blessed with this boon, Maninaga started to wander around freely. Although Garuda could not kill Maninaga, he captured him and kept him imprisoned in his own house.

Shiva had a companion named Nandi. Nandi asked Shiva, "Lord, what has happened to Maninaga? We have not seen him for some time. Has Garuda done him some harm?"

Shiva of course knew what had happened. He advised Nandi to pray to Vishnu. Nandi was to please Vishnu and then ask for the boon that Maninaga might be freed from Garuda's imprisonment. Nandi did this and Vishnu asked Garuda to release Maninaga. But Garuda refused. "This is not right. You ride me when you go out to fight the demons. They get defeated because of my prowess."

89. *Vishnu and Garuda*

Vishnu smiled and replied, "Garuda, you are quite right. You have become thin and lean from bearing my weight. You have a lot of strength. Why don't you bear the weight of my little finger and demonstrate your strength?"

Vishnu placed his little finger on Garuda's head. So heavy was the finger that Garuda was crushed against the ground. "Please forgive me," said Garuda.

Vishnu asked Nandi to take Garuda to Shiva. Shiva would find a way of restoring Garuda's old appearance. Maninaga was released and Nandi took Garuda to Shiva. Shiva asked Garuda to bathe in Gautami Ganga (Gomti River). This would make his appearance normal again. Garuda did this. Not only was his old appearance restored, but also he became stronger and swifter than he used to be. The place where Garuda bathed got converted into a tirtha known as Garuda-tirtha.

90. *Arrogant Mount Vindhya*

Once during Narada's travels, he came to Mount Vindhya. Narada told Mount Vindhya that Mount Meru was superior. "Meru stands so tall that Surya shines on his peaks. Kailasa, the abode of Shiva, is at his feet. You are so simple and humble." Mount Vindhya was now taken over by jealousy. He asked Surya to go round him rather than around Meru. But Surya refused. Vindhya raised his peaks up and blocked the Sun's usual route. One side of the Earth got no sunlight. The other side got scorched. The gods appealed to Shiva, who asked them to appeal to Vishnu. "Only Sage Agastya can help you," said Vishnu. The gods now appealed to Sage Agastya. The old sage went to his disciple Vindhya who bowed his head to his Guru.

"Wait for me like this," said his Guru, "till I come back from my visit to the south." Sage Agastya never came back and Vindhya stood there with his head bent. The Sun's path was no longer blocked.

91. *What is Maya?*

Once, a poor Brahmana named Somasharma of Haridwar pondered what Maya was. He was totally committed to worshipping Lord Vishnu. His mind was filled with numerous questions concerning life. "I occasionally hear that life is an illusion or Maya. What is this Maya?" he asked Vishnu.

"Go and take a bath in the nearby stream," Vishnu told him. Somasharma put down his things and clothes and plunged in. The very next moment, he changed into a Nishada woman. He became a woman of a forest tribe that hunted birds and small animals. He was married to a tribal man and had seven children. He had lost all the recollection of being Somasharma. Suddenly, he saw Vishnu standing in front of her. "Go and take a dip in that stream." The tribal woman took off her simple clothes and took a plunge.

92. *Maya is Banished*

The very next moment, Somasharma regained his original form by the riverside. His clothes, water-pot and stick were still lying there. His old friends– the Brahmanas and the sages at Haridwar– were around him. They asked, "Why did you take so long today to bathe?"

Though Somasharma realised he was back in his old life, he also mulled over the new life he had as a tribal woman–a life that was now an old one for him. He saw the simple tribal man crying, "Oh, my wife is dead!" "This is the Maya you requested an explanation of. Now, can you see? The pleasures and tragedies of our family life are all Maya. It appears to be present. However, as soon as Maya is banished, it disappears. Human beings cannot comprehend all that is divine, such as Maya," said Vishnu.

93. *Shiva in the Devadaru Forest*

Deva means god and daru means tree (or wood). A devadaru is a special sort of tree (a sort of pine tree) that is loved by the gods.

In a devadaru forest, there lived many sages with their wives. The sages were devoted to Lord Shiva and performed austere penance so as to please him. Shiva was pleased at their prayers. But he decided to test the sages. He, therefore, put on a very ugly appearance and came to the devadaru forest. He wore no clothes; his complexion was completely dark and his eyes were terrifying. The wives of the sages began to follow Shiva around. But the sages were disgusted that their wives should follow such an ugly and deformed creature. They used many harsh words to insult Shiva and as a result, Shiva promptly disappeared.

The sages then went and reported what had happened to Brahma.

94. *Sage Sudarshana*

Brahma said, "Don't you realise what you have done? That ugly creature was none other than Shiva himself. He was merely trying to test you. A guest is a guest regardless of whether he is handsome or ugly. He must be treated with utmost respect. Don't you know the story of Sage Sudarshana?

"The great Sage Sudarshana took pains to instruct his wife that a guest must always be treated well and must never be refused. On one particular occasion, the god of righteousness, Dharma, desired to test Sudarshana and his wife. He adopted the disguise of a Brahmana and came to visit Sudarshana. Sudarshana was away at that time, but his wife treated the guest really well. Dharma then blessed Sudarshana and his wife that they would surely go to heaven."

The sages regretted what they had done. They sought Brahma's advice and Brahma told them the story of Shveta.

95. *Shveta, Devotee of Shiva*

There was a poor but learned man named Shveta who was a great devotee of Shiva. He lived in a little hut by the river Gautami and worshipped Shiva all day.

Yama's records indicated the day for his death. Yama sent down his Yamadootas or messengers to fetch Shveta. But they could not even enter Shveta's house. Yama now sent his companion Mrityu (death) to find out what was going on. Mrityu went to Shveta's house and found Yama's messengers standing outside the house. Mrityu flung a noose to grasp Shveta's body. Nandi brought him down.

Yama himself came along with his soldiers. Nandi, Ganesha, Karttikeya and several of Shiva's companions came to fight and a royal battle raged. Yama was, after all, performing his duty. But Shiva insisted that his devotee would never be taken to Yama, but would instead go straight to heaven. Shiva's condition was finally agreed to.

96. *Shiva Teaches about Bhasma*

Brahma told the sages thus, "Now you know what can be gained by praying to Shiva. That is what you should do."

That is what the sages did. After they had prayed faithfully for an entire year, Shiva appeared before them. He was smeared with ashes and his visage was terrible. He wandered around the devadaru forest. But the sages had learnt their lesson. They were not disgusted with Shiva's ugly appearance. They with their wives welcomed Shiva with flowers and incense.

Shiva was pleased. He gave the sages plenty of good advice. Amongst other things, he taught the sages the wonderful properties of bhasma (ashes).

97. *The Sacrifice of Dadhichi*

Dadhichi was the son of Sage Atharvan and his wife Chitti. Once, an Asura named Vritra defeated all the gods and became the king of heaven. The gods could not defeat him with any weapon. Vritra also took all the water on the earth and caused havoc.

Indra approached Vishnu for his help in defeating Vritra. Vishnu told Indra that only a weapon made of bones of Sage Dadhichi could kill Vritra.

The devas, therefore, went to request the sage for his bones. Sage Dadhichi told them that everyone dies one day, so why not die for a good cause? He killed his body with yoga vidya and the devas made a weapon called Vajra with the bones.

Indra challenged Vritra for war and killed him with Vajra. The devas and people on the earth were saved by this great sacrifice of Sage Dadhichi.

98. *Rudraksha, the Tears of Shiva*

Rudraksha comprises two words, 'Rudra' and 'aksha'. 'Rudra' signifies Shiva, and 'aksha' stands for tears. Lord Shiva himself is the first ardent user and admirer of Rudraksha.

The Shiva Purana mentions story about how Rudraksha beads came into existence. The berries of Rudraksha symbolise Rudra's sacred tears that dribbled down his cheeks after he had returned from his deep meditational state. The tears fell on the earth and turned into seeds out of which Rudraksha trees grew. Later, devotees and sages began using Rudraksha as a blessing from Lord Shiva to protect mankind from worldly sufferings and miseries.

In the Shiva Purana, Lord Shiva himself states, "A person who wears Rudraksha becomes like Me. So, a human being should try to wear Rudraksha."

99. *Arjuna at Indrakeela*

In the Mahabharata war, many divyastras (divine weapons) were used. To obtain a divyastra, one had to undergo great penance and sacrifice and be blessed by the Devas.

Yudhishthira, the eldest of the Pandavas, knew that only Arjuna among them could master and be blessed with the divyastras. So, he advised Arjuna to perform penance and attain the divine weapons. Arjuna went to Indrakeela mountain to perform tapasya. There, his divine father Indra appeared before him and advised him to please Shiva and obtain the Pashupatastra from him. Arjuna performed austere penance to please Shiva. Pleased by Arjuna, Shiva and Parvati disguised as hunter, a Kirata, and huntress, along with the ganas came to indrakeela mountain. At that very time, Mukasura appeared to kill Arjuna. He appeared in the form of a wild boar. Arjuna aimed an arrow at the boar. The arrow hit the boar. But surprisingly, another arrow too had hit the boar with so much ferociousness that Mukasura died instantly.

100. *Arjuna's Combat with the Kirata*

Both Arjuna and the Kirata staked their claim over the boar. A fight broke out between Arjuna and the Kirata about who would take the boar. When the two got into a wrestling bout, the Kirata started to choke Arjuna.

During the interval, Arjuna promptly started pleading with Shiva for assistance. He took a handful of clay and made a tiny figure of Shiva. After picking some flowers, he created a garland. Then he threw it at the statue. The garland dropped around the Kirata's neck.

Arjuna recognised that the hunter was actually Lord Shiva whom he was worshipping. He was not a local hunter. Shiva was testing Arjuna. Soon Shiva and Parvati took their original forms and handed over the Pashupatastra to Arjuna and blessed him.

101. *The Ketaki Flower*

The Shiva Purana tells us why the ketaki flower is not used to worship Shiva. Rama, Lakshmana and Sita were spending their exile. They had just received the news of Dasharatha's death. Rama as the eldest son decided to perform the funeral rights in the forest. He sent Lakshmana to get the required materials. Lakshmana did not return for a long time. So, Rama set out to find him. It was nearing afternoon and both Rama and Lakshmana had not returned. Sita decided to do the funeral rites herself. Two disembodied hands appeared and claimed to be Dashratha. They accepted the offering. Sita said that Rama and Lakshmana would not believe her. The hands said that the river Phalgu, Agni, a cow standing near by and a ketaki flower would be the witnesses.

102. *The Curse*

Rama and Lakshmana returned with all the materials and sat down for the offerings. Sita said, "I have already made the offerings and your ancestors have come and accepted them." Rama and Lakshmana did not believe her.

Sita asked all the four witnesses, but they did not speak and kept quiet. When Rama and Lakshmana started performing the rites, a voice from heaven explained that Sita had already completed it. Then Surya, the Sun-god, himself came forward as Sita's witness. Sita was angry with the witnesses. She cursed the Phalgu river that it would flow only underground. Agni would consume all things irrespective of what it was. The cow's mouth would become impure because it had lied through that. Lastly, the ketaki flower would never be used to worship Shiva.

103. *King Kalmashpada and Shakti*

King Kalmashpada, son of Saudasa, was born in the Ikshvaku dynasty. Sage Vashishtha was his priest. One day, the king holding a sacrifice invited Sage Vashishtha. Being busy, the sage refused. Angry, the king decided to call Sage Vishwamitra. He went to invite Vishwamitra and on his way back along with Vishwamitra, they came across Shakti, son of Vashishtha. As the path was narrow, the king asked Shakti to give way. Shakti said, as a Brahmana, he needed to go first. Both started quarrelling. None of them was willing to give way. The king was angry and struck Shakti with a whip.

Angry Shakti cursed the king. "You are nothing short of a Rakshasa! Go and turn into one." The king turned into a demon. He killed Shakti and ate him up. Having eaten up Shakti, he became terrible in form. Vishwamitra took the king now to the place where Vashishtha's hundred sons were. Seeing the sons, the king ate them up as well.

104. *Vashishtha's Sorrow*

Vashishtha was not there at that time. When he came home, he saw an empty house. Meditating, he realised that Vishwamitra was the cause of all this. Saddened, he wanted to kill himself.

Suddenly, he heard someone reciting the Vedas and also calling him. Turning, he saw Shakti's wife. He asked her who was reciting the Vedas. The woman said that it was her unborn child. Vashishtha felt happy.

One day, Vashishtha came across king Kalmashpada who was eating human flesh. Seeing the sage, the king rushed to eat him. Vashishtha sprinkled some water from the pot he was carrying. The spirit that had possessed the king left, and the king was back to normal. Regaining consciousness, the king fell at Vashishtha's feet and begged for forgiveness. The sage forgave him and the king left.

105. *King Nimi*

King Nimi was the forefather of King Janaka. He was a descendant of Ikshvaku. Once, he decided to perform a yajna lasting for a full thousand years. He went to Sage Vashishtha and asked him to perform the yajna. But the Sage refused as he was already engaged in performing a yajna arranged by Indra. This yajna was to last for 500 years. So, the sage advised Nimi to wait and promised to join his ceremony as soon as his commitment to Indra was over.

Hearing this, Nimi returned with the impression that the Sage would join his yajna as soon as he was free, while Vashishtha thought that Nimi would wait for his arrival and only then would he start yajna. The result was that Nimi conducted the yajna with the help of the other sages. Meanwhile, after completing the yajna that Indra had arranged, Vashishtha came to Nimi's place to start the yajna. But to his dismay, he found that the yajna had already begun.

106. *King of the Blink*

Sage Vashishtha felt insulted and cursed the king that he would henceforth be without a body (videha). In retaliation, the king also cursed Vashishtha that, henceforth, he too would be without a body. However, the curse of Nimi did not have any lasting effect on Vashishtha. But Nimi became without a body. Meanwhile, the yajna continued. When the ceremony was over, the gods promised to give Nimi a new body. But the king found himself having a universal vision with his body gone. So, he requested the gods that he might be allowed to live on the eyelids of all living beings. The boon was eventually granted to him. It is believed that since then, Nimi has been living on the eyelids of all beings and the blinking of the eye is called 'nimesha'. His son came to be called 'Vaideha'. Sita was the daughter of Vaideha (Janak) and so was called Vaidehi.

107. *Sage Richika*

Gadhi, the king of Kanyakubja, had a daughter named Satyavati. Sage Richika, descendant of Sage Bhrigu, wanted to marry Satyavati. But Gadhi had no desire to marry off his daughter to an old Brahmana who was also very short-tempered. So, he demanded one thousand horses white in colour with black ears. Sage Richika managed to get such horses from Varuna and thus married Satyavati.

Satyavati wanted a son. So, Sage Richika performed a yajna and obtained some rice pudding as a result. But Satyavati wished that her mother might also have a son. The sage, therefore, prepared a second bowl of rice pudding. He gave the two bowls to Satyavati and said, "This is for you and this for your mother." He then went off to the forest. Satyavati's mother deceived her daughter. According to her mother's order, Satyavati gave her bowl to her mother and herself ate from her mother's bowl.

108. *Satyavati's Son and Grandson*

Sage Richika came back from the forest and heard what had happened. He was very angry. Into the bowl of Satyavati's mother he had put the ingredients for a son who would be brave and violent as a Kshatriya should be. And into Satyavati's bowl, he had put the ingredients for a son who would be peaceful and non-violent as a Brahmana should be. Everything had now been reversed.

Hearing this, Satyavati became sad and started crying. She said, "I don't want to be a mother of a son of Kshatriya quality. May my grandson be a man of this quality!" Sage Richika granted this boon. As a result, Satyavati became the mother of the great sage Jamadagni. But the grandson of Richika and the son of Jamadagni was Parasurama who was quite powerful and ferocious. On the other side, Satyavati's mother gave birth to his son Visvamitra, who became Brahmarishi in his later life.

109. *Rishi Chyavana and Princess Sukanya*

The Bhagavata Purana tells the story of Sage Chyavana who was the son of Bhrigu Maharshi and his wife Pauloma. Once while Chyavana was performing tapa, he was fully covered with anthill except his eyes. By this time, a young princess named Sukanya, the daughter of King Sharyati, entered into the forest. She felt that the shining eyes were glittering worms and so she poped at them, causing Sage Chyavana a blind man.

The Sage cursed that the soldiers of the King would suffer from the stoppage of their body excrements. The King approached the blinded Sage and offered his daughter in wedding to take care of the Sage.

Princess Sukanya was thus given in marriage to the Sage; she left the palace and moved to the forest hermitage of Sage Chayavana. One day, the Ashwini Kumaras, sons of Lord Surya, and royal physicians of heaven, came by the hermitage. They were attracted to the beauty of Sukanya.

110. *Sukanya, the Dedicated Princess*

The Ashwini Kumaras asked Sukanya to take one of them as her husband. But Sukanya was very loyal, devoted and chaste. When the persuasions failed, the Ashwini Kumaras told her that her husband Sage Chyavana would restore her youth and beauty by taking a bath along with them. Chyavana accepted to take a bath with the Ashwini Kumaras.

The three bathed in a pond and came forth with celestial beauty. The three of them looked alike and claimed to be the real Sage Chyavana. Each one asked her to be his bride. By the power of chastity, Sukanya recognised and chose her own husband. The Ashwini Kumaras were, in fact, testing the chastity of Sukanya; now she had won all the tests. Sage Chyavana gave a boon in turn to the Ashwini Kumaras that they would become eligible to receive havis (oblation offered to gods) from yajnas which was denied to them by Indra.

111. *King Ambarisha and Sage Durvasa*

King Ambarisha was a great devotee of Lord Vishnu. Lord Vishnu blessed the king with his Sudarshan Chakra. Once, king Ambarisha performed Ekadashi Vrata. The fast would be broken on Dwadashi (12th day). On one such Dwadashi day, Sage Durvasa came to meet king Ambarisha. The king welcomed him and requested him to join him for food. Sage Durvasa said that he would join him for the food only after taking his bath. The sage seemed to be taking a long time to come back. The king decided that he would break the fast by having a small quantity of water.

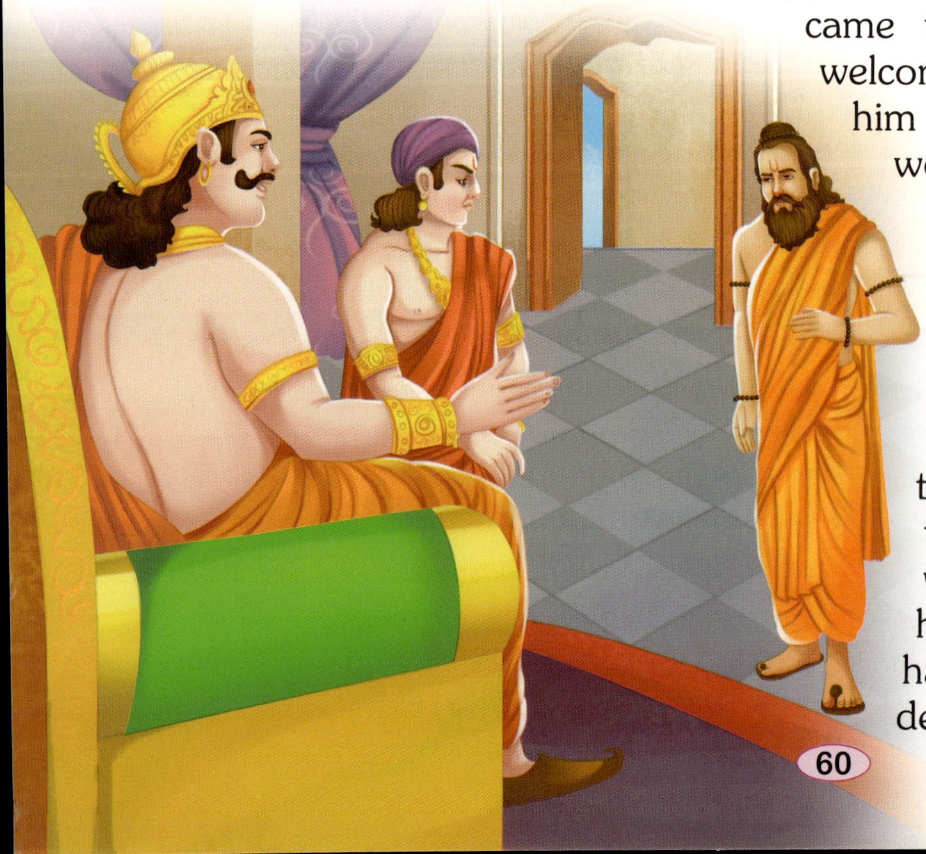

Soon thereafter, the sage reached the palace. He was furious and chastised the king for disrespecting him by not waiting for the guest before breaking his fast. He plucked out a strand of hair from his head and created a huge demon named Krucha to kill the king.

112. *Durvasa is Forgiven*

As the demon charged at king Ambarisha, the king prayed to Lord Vishnu to protect him. When the demon was about to attack the king, a whirring sound came from above. It was the Sudarshana Chakra of Lord Vishnu. In no time, the demon was killed and the divine Chakra then directed its attention to Durvasa. He started running for his life but the Chakra never stopped chasing him. He first approached Lord Brahma and then Lord Shiva with a request to save him.

Both of them expressed their helplessness. When the sage approached Lord Vishnu, he was told that only king Ambarisha himself could save him from this predicament. He then approached the king and asked for forgiveness. The king prayed to Lord Vishnu to forgive the sage. Immediately, the Chakra stopped and disappeared. Thus the sage was relieved of his distress.

113. *King Rantideva*

Long ago, there lived King Rantideva. He was a great devotee of Lord Vishnu. He served anyone who came to him for help. In due course, all of Rantideva's wealth got spent. Rantideva starved for days and prayed to Lord Vishnu.

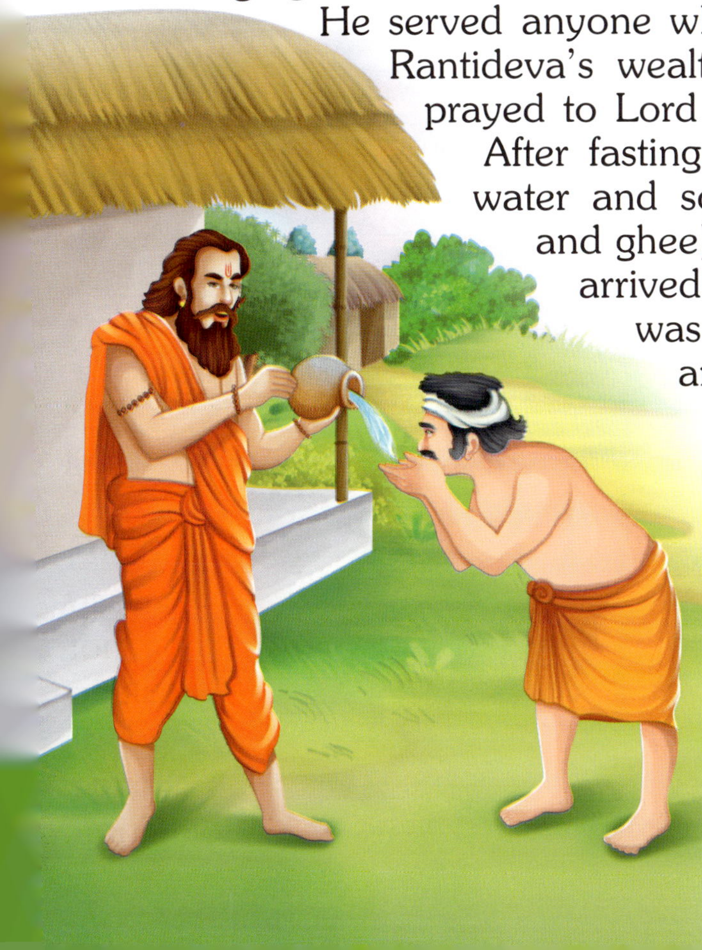

After fasting for forty-eight days, Rantideva received some water and some paramaannam (paayasam with rice, milk and ghee). Just when he was about to eat it, a Brahmana arrived. He gave him a share. Thereafter, Rantideva was just about to eat his own share when a Shudra arrived. Rantideva gave him also his share. Then, a man arrived, surrounded by dogs. Rantideva offered the remaining portion to him. When the king was just about to drink water, a chandaala appeared.

Rantideva gave it to the chandaala. The Trinity of gods appeared before Rantideva. They revealed that they had come in the forms of the Brahmana, Shudra and Chandaala in order to test him. Lord Vishnu granted the king salvation.

114. *Ajamila*

Ajamila was a pious and religious Brahmin. One day, when he was collecting wood from the forest for his ritual purposes, he came across a beautiful woman and immediately fell for her beauty. His lust for the lady, who was a prostitute, distracted him completely from his earlier pious life. He abandoned his family, his rituals and practices, and started living with her.

Many years later, when it was time for him to leave this mortal world, the Yamadootas came to him and told him that his time was up and that they were going to tie their noose around him and take him to Naraka (hell) for all his sins. Hearing this, Ajamila was very scared.

Sensing his end was near, he wanted to see his son one last time as he had immense affection for him. Fortunately, he had named his son Narayana. At this sorrowful time, he called out aloud to his son.

115. *The Deliverance of Ajamila*

There appeared four divine beings. These divine beings stopped the Yamadootas. Upon enquiry by the Yamadootas, the divine beings introduced themselves as the Vishnudootas. A quarrel ensued between the two sets of messengers.

The Vishnudootas said, "Ajamila has already atoned not only for sins committed in one life but also for those committed in millions of lives, for he chanted the holy name of Narayana in a helpless condition. Simply by chanting the name of Narayana in this way, he sufficiently atoned for the sinful acts done in millions of lives." Meanwhile, Ajamila realised how powerful and merciful the name of Narayana is. He repented for his sins. He immediately left the lowly life that he was living until then and went back to his family. Thereafter, he lived a pious life, devoted to Narayana.

116. *Vahanas, the Vehicles of Gods and Goddesses*

All the gods and the goddesses travel using specific animals and birds. Vahanas are the names given to these modes of transport. These divine vehicles represent many spiritual and psychological forces.

The three godheads Brahma, Vishnu and Maheshwara use the Swan, the Garuda, and the Bull respectively. Indra uses the Horse, the Elephant, and also the horse-chariot driven by the charioteer Matali. Surya has his chariot pulled by the Saptashva or Seven Horses. Chandra uses an Antelope, Agni uses a Ram, and Poosha uses a Goat. Yama rides a Water Buffalo. Varuna uses a Crocodile and a Tortoise. Shanideva uses the Vulture and the Crow. Durga rides a Lion, Ganga's mount is the Crocodile, Yamuna's mount is the Tortoise, and Sarasvati's, the Swan. Lakshmi flies on the Owl.

117. *Mushika, Ganesha's Vahana*

Once, there was a Gandharva (a celestial being) named Kroncha. In the court of Indra, he met Sage Vamadeva. Filled with pride, he insulted the sage.

This incited the anger of the sage, who cursed him that he would become a mouse. Kroncha turned into a mouse, and entered the ashrama of Sage Parashara. He started creating havoc. Meanwhile, Ganesha was paying a visit to the sage. Ganesha at once realised the true identity of the mouse. Using a rope, he lassoed the mouse, and mounted it. Contact with the divine body of Ganesha made Kroncha at last realise the error he had made. Besides, Ganesha was so heavy that he felt himself being crushed. He prayed to Ganesha, "Lord, please forgive me for my sins. Please accept me as your mount and release me from this misery!" Ganesha made himself light enough for the mouse to bear his weight. And thus did he become Mushika Vahana.

118. *Nandi, Son of Shilada*

Once, there was a sage named Shilada who was a great devotee of Lord Shiva. He had no children. So, he prayed to Shiva for many years for a child. Finally, Shiva granted his wish.

The next day, Shilada found a baby-boy who was shining as bright as the sun himself. Then a voice from the sky was heard instructing Shilada to take care of the son. Shilada took the son home and named him Nandi. Shilada took care of the child. He showered upon him lots of love and affection. Nandi grew to be very wise and intelligent. He was devoted to Shiva. He would spend his days meditating on Shiva and chanting his name.

Some years later, two sages, Mitra and Varuna, came to Shilada's home. Shilada noticed that the sages blessed Nandi only half-heartedly. The sages explained that the fate of Nandi was written in such a way that he could not lead a very long life. Shilada was heart-broken but Nandi was not scared.

119. *Nandi Becomes Shiva's Vahana*

One day, Nandi was meditating in the forest when Shiva appeared before him. Shiva was very pleased with Nandi's devotion. He asked Nandi to seek the boon of his choice. "Lord, I wish to be with you always," said Nandi.

Shiva smiled. "Nandi, I have just lost my bull, which I used to ride. Henceforth, you shall have the face of a bull. You shall stay in my home at Mount Kailasa. You shall be the head of all my Ganas and you shall be my companion, my vehicle and my friend, always!" Nandi closed his eyes as tears flowed through them. The Lord had granted him his wish. Since then, Nandi became Shiva's vehicle, doorman, his companion and the head of all of his attendants, the Ganas.

120. *Ravana and the Pushpaka Vimana*

The Pushpaka Vimana was built by the divine architect Vishwakarma for Brahma, who then gifted it to Kubera, the god of wealth. But the Vimana was later stolen, along with Lanka, by Kubera's half-brother, the demon-king Ravana.

After defeating his elder brother Kubera, Ravana passed through Mount Kailasa in the Pushpaka Vimana. There, Ravana got into a fight with Shiva's attendant Nandi. Puffed up with arrogance, Ravana lifted Mount Kailasa that trembled goddess Parvati and other ganas. Shiva pressed the mountain by his toe. That struck Ravana's hands. It is because of this incident that he came to be called Ravana, the Noisy one. In pain, Ravana asked for forgiveness and praised Shiva. Shiva relaxed the pressure on Mount Kailasa, and, therefore, upon Ravana. Shiva pleased with him gave him Chandrahas sword and Ravana flew back to Lanka.

121. *Kali Kills Raktabija*

Once, there was a demon named Raktabija. He had been given a boon by Lord Brahma. Every drop of his blood that touched the ground transformed itself into another demon. So, whenever he was attacked and harmed, more Raktabijas were born.

In despair, the gods turned to Lord Shiva. But Shiva was lost in meditation, so they turned to his consort Parvati. The goddess set out in the form of Kali. In this terrible form, she cut off Raktabija's head.

Kali then spread her tongue to cover the battlefield preventing even a single drop of Raktabija's blood from falling on the ground. With mouth, tongue and chest all bloodied, she began to dance on the battlefield. To stop her, Shiva lay down upon the battlefield. She stepped upon her own husband. Shocked at this sight, Kali stuck out her tongue in astonishment. Hence, one can see the common image of Kali, standing with one foot on Shiva's chest, with her enormous tongue stuck out.

122. *Parikshit is Cursed*

Parikshit, born to Abhimanyu (son of the third Pandava Arjuna) and Uttara, was a just and great ruler. One day, while he along with his soldiers were on a hunt, chasing a deer, he came across Sameeka, a sage deep in his meditation. Parikshit asked the sage about the deer. But he was angry upon receiving no reply. He hung a dead snake around the sage's neck and left. Shringi, Sameeka's son, saw his father sitting with a dead snake around his neck. He cursed the person who had done the insulting act. He cursed, "Within seven days, may the great poisonous snake Takshaka bite the one who has insulted my father!"

Parikshit, upon coming to know his fate, was filled with remorse and fear. He prepared a special guarded house to live in. Takshaka disguised himself in a fruit basket was sent to Parikshit by some snakes posing as Brahmanas. He bit Parikshit at sunset of the seventh day, thus killing him.

123. *Krishna and Sage Utanka*

After the Great War of the Mahabharata was over, Krishna was travelling back to Dwaraka. On his way back, he passed a barren desert. He waited there for the night. There, in the barren desert, he met a sage named Utanka. Utanka was a great devotee of Lord Vishnu. He spent most of his time in meditation and did not know much about what happened in the outer world.

Utanka asked Krishna if he was able to prevent the war between the Kauravas and the Pandavas. After all, Krishna was the Lord of the Universe and everything was possible for him. Utanka had great hope that Krishna would be able to prevent the great killings that would otherwise result from the bitter enmity between the Kauravas and the Pandavas. Krishna told Utanka that he tried his best to prevent the war but to no avail. Utanka became angry with Krishna.

124. *Utanka Sees Krishna's Vishvarupa*

Krishna told Utanka that he went on a peace mission to the Kauravas, even asked them for five villages, but the Kauravas did not listen at all. He told Utanka that what is lotted can't be blotted. The Kauravas were supposed to reap the fruits of their evil actions. Hence, they were destroyed. Only the five Pandavas were alive because they were following the path of Dharma.

Hearing this, Utanka became more angry. Krishna told him that he also showed the Kauravas his true form– the Vishvarupa. But the Kauravas thought it to be black magic. The Kauravas were destroyed by their own karma.

Utanka understood everything. He wanted to see the Universal Form of Krishna. Krishna showed him his Vishvarupa that he had shown to Arjuna in the beginning of the great battle. Krishna then asked Utanka for a boon. Utanka asked for a Siddhi by virtue of that he, staying in a desert, should be able to get water whenever he wanted. Krishna granted him the boon.

125. *Samjna, the Wife of Surya*

Sage Kashyapa and his wife Aditi had a son named Vivasvana. He was very bright and was thus known as the Sun-god or Surya. Surya was married to Samjna, Vishvakarma's daughter. They had two sons, Vaivasvata Manu and Yamadharma, the god of death. Yama had a twin sister named Yami.

Samjna loved her husband very much. Since Surya's energy was intolerable, Samjna could not stay with him for long or look at him. So, she created a woman out of her own Chhaya or shadow. She instructed her to take her place.

Samjna told Chhaya, "I cannot bear the energy of my husband, so I am going off to my father's house. Stay here, pretend to be myself before my husband and take care of my children. Under no circumstances tell nobody, especially my husband, that you are not Samjna." Chhaya promised to keep quiet as long as she was not cursed for it.

126. *Chhaya Reveals the Truth*

Samjna went to her father's house. Her father Vishvakarma asked her to return to Surya. But she went to a place, known as Uttara Kuru, disguised herself and lived there as a mare.

Surya had not realised that Samjna had been replaced by Chhaya. He had three children born through Chhaya: two sons, Shrutashravas and Shrutakarma, and a daughter Tapati. As soon as Chhaya had her own children, she no longer cared for Samjna's children. Vaivasvata Manu, the elder son, was very quiet. But Yama was not so tolerant. One day, he raised his leg to kick Chhaya. At this, Chhaya cursed Yama that his legs would fall off.

Yama went and complained to Surya. "I have not really kicked her," he said, "I only threatened to do so. And does a mother can ever curse her children like this?" Surya felt that there was some truth in what Yama uttered. He questioned his wife. Chhaya revealed the truth.

127. *Resizing the Sun*

Chhaya's truth shocked Surya. He told Yama, "I can't fully undo the curse. I can reduce its severity. Your legs will not actually fall off. Some of the flesh from your legs will fall off onto the earth and create worms." In an angry mood, Surya went to Vishvakarma's house. Vishvakarma then advised Surya, "It all happened because of your excess energy. If you permit, I will remove some of the extra energy. Then Samjna will be able to look at you."

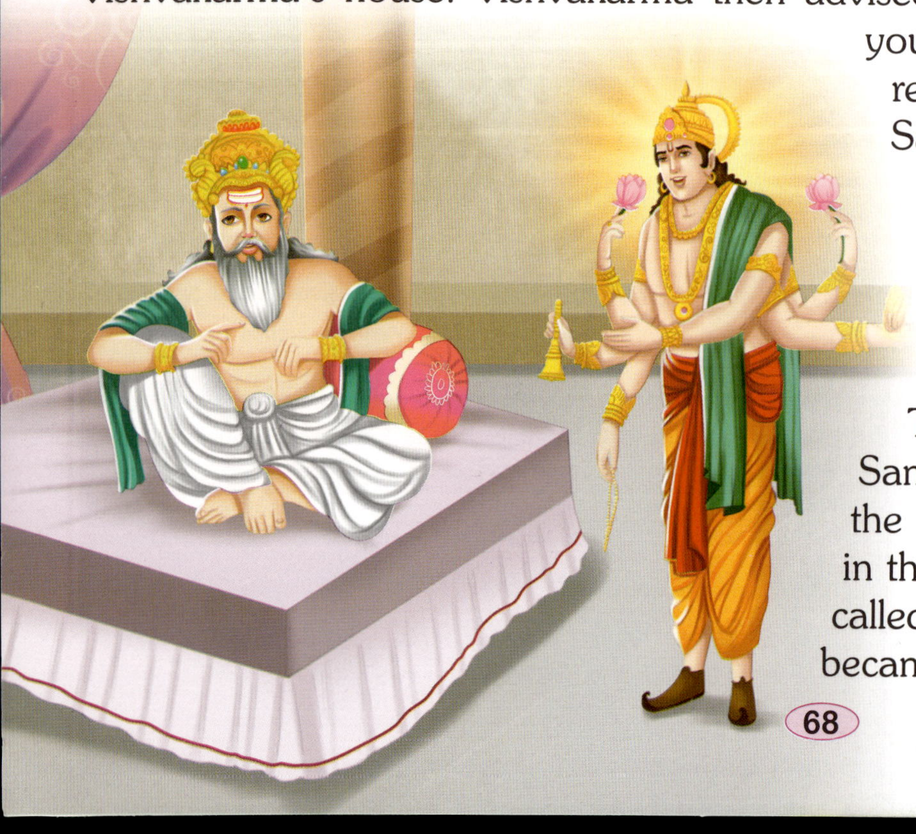

Surya agreed and Viswakarma chipped off the excess energy of Sun. With the removed energy, Vishvakarma created Vishnu's chakra (bladed discus).

Then Surya went in search of his wife Samjna and found her in Uttara Kuru in the form of a mare. He joined her there in the form of a horse. They had two sons called Ashvini Kumaras. Both of them later became the royal physicians of the gods.

128. *Manikundala and Goutama*

In the city of Bhouvana, there lived a Brahmana named Goutama. The Brahmana had a vaishya (trading class) friend named Manikundala.

Goutama was greedy and dishonest. Manikundala was simple by nature. Goutama wanted Manikundala's wealth. He made him run away from home with all his wealth, without telling anyone.

In the course of their travel, Goutama remarked, "Have you noticed how those who follow the path of Dharma (righteousness) always suffer? They are neither wealthy nor happy. There seems to be no point in being righteous."

"Please don't say that," protested Manikundala, "Happiness lies in following the path of Dharma." The two friends argued over this, but could not decide who was right. They resolved to have a bet. They would ask the opinions of others. And whoever lost the bet would surrender all his wealth to the winner.

129. *Manikundala Praises Dharma*

Manikundala and Goutama asked many people for their opinions. Most people said that it was the evil who thrived and prospered. And it was the righteous who suffered. As per the agreement, Manikundala lost all this wealth to Goutama. But he continued to sing the praise of Dharma.

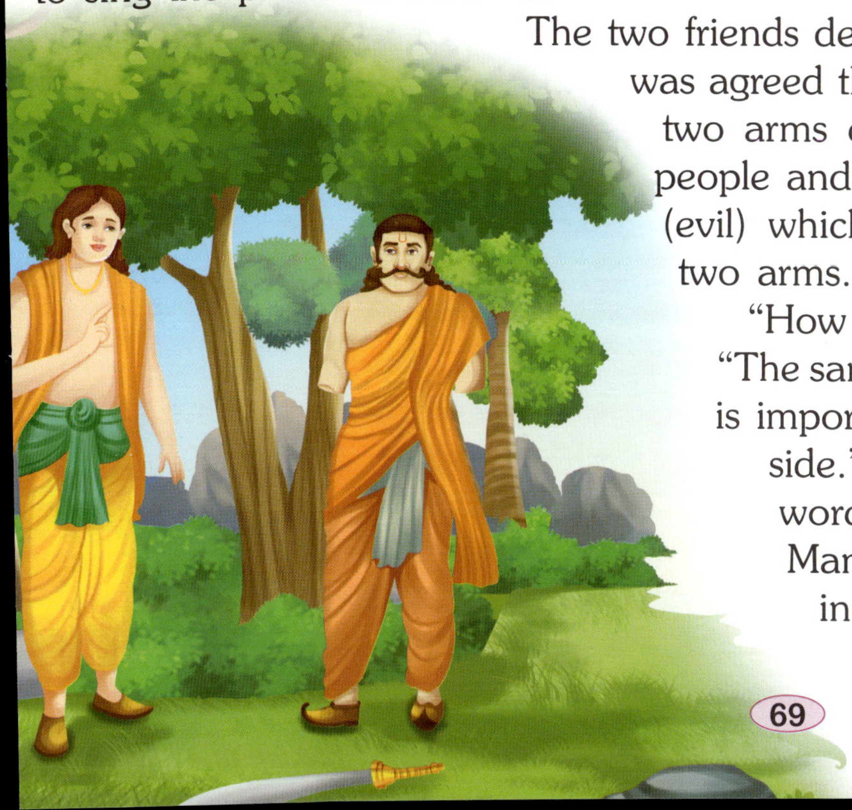

The two friends decided to have another bet. This time, it was agreed that whoever lost the bet would have his two arms chopped off. They again asked several people and most people said that it was Adharma (evil) which triumphed. So, Manikundala lost his two arms.

"How does it feel now?" asked Goutama. "The same as ever," replied Manikundala. "What is important is Dharma. And Dharma is on my side." Goutama lost his temper hearing the words of his friend. He threatened to cut off Manikundala's head if Manikundala persisted in his praise of Dharma. But Manikundala was unperturbed.

130. *Dharma or Adharma?*

The two friends decided to have another bet. This time, whoever lost would forfeit his life. Manikundala lost once again. And Goutama gouged out Manikundala's eyes and left him. Manikundala lay on the banks of the Goutami Ganga.

There was an image of Lord Vishnu on the banks of the river and demon Vibhishana used to come there every night to pray to Vishnu. Vibhishana's son discovered Manikundala lying there and found out from him the entire story. He recounted the story to his father.

"Many years ago, I had joined Rama in his fight with Ravana," Vibhishana told his son, "Ravana's son Meghanada shot a venomous arrow at Rama's brother Lakshmana. Lakshmana fell unconscious. Hanuman had fetched the Gandhamadana hill with Vishalyakarani and Mritasanjeevani herbs growing on it, to revive Lakshmana. On his way to put the hill back, he had passed this area and dropped some broken bits of herbs here. They had taken root. Let us find it."

131. *Dharma Restored*

Father and son hunted for the herb. The Vishalyakarani had become a huge tree. They lopped off a branch and placed it on Manikundala's chest. Manikundala immediately regained his eyes and arms. After curing Manikundala, Vibhishana and his retinue returned to Lanka. Manikundala was on his way. He eventually reached a city named Mahapura where a king named Maharaja ruled. Maharaja had no sons and a daughter. The daughter was blind. Maharaja had announced that whoever cured his daughter would become his son-in-law and rule after him. Manikundala cured the princess with Vishalyakarani. He then married the princess and became the king of Mahapura.

Many years later, Goutama was brought before Manikundala by the soldiers. He had been arrested on the charge of committing a crime. Goutama had lost all his wealth by then. Manikundala pardoned his friend and shared with him whatever he had. Such are the virtues of following the path of Dharma.

132. *Dhruva*

The Bhagavata Purana mentions the story of Dhruva. To continue with the process of creation, Lord Brahma gave birth to a man and a woman from his own body. The man was named Svayambhuva Manu and the woman was named Shatarupa. Humans descended from Manu. That is the reason they are known as manava. Manu and Shatarupa had three sons named Vira, Priyavrata and Uttanapada.

Uttanapada became a king and lived with his two wives Suniti and Suruchi. Suruchi, being the younger wife, was the favourite of the king. Suniti had a child Dhruva and Suruchi's son was named Uttama. One day, when Uttanapada was seated on his throne, Uttama climbed up his lap to play with his father. Suruchi was standing near by. Dhruva too wanted to climb onto the king's lap. Suruchi got furious and pushed Dhruva away.

133. *Dhruva's Penance*

Suruchi said, "You are not fit to sit on your father's lap. Go to the jungle and pray to Sri Hari to make you my son in your next birth. Then, you can sit on your father's lap." Dhruva was hurt. With his eyes full of tears, he ran to his mother's room. Suniti was aghast at seeing the sobbing child. "Pray to Hari or Vishnu," said Suniti, "He alone can remove your sorrow." Dhruva left home searching for Vishnu.

Sage Narada chanced to see him. He stopped Dhruva and asked what happened. Sage Narada tried to dissuade him from going to the jungle. But Dhruva had made up his mind. Narada was astonished at the determination of Dhruva and told him to go to Madhu Vana near the river Yamuna and perform his penance.

134. *Dhruva Sees Hari*

In the first month, Dhruva lived on some fruits. In the next month, it was leaves and in six months, he had controlled his hunger and stood on one leg, with eyes closed meditating upon the glorious form of Sri Hari. One day, Dhruva opened his eyes and to his joy found Sri Hari looking at him. "What do you want, my child?" Vishnu asked in a sympathetic tone.

Dhruva realised that he had forgotten everything he wanted to ask Vishnu. "I want to remain with you forever, my Lord," he said. Sri Hari said, "Dhruva, I know the purpose for which you came here to meditate. Now, you go back to your palace with no fear. After your tenure is over on this earth, you shall come to me and I will give you a place where nobody can reach you. Go, my child; go back!" Dhruva got up and Sri Hari vanished.

135. *Dhruva Tara*

As soon as Dhruva had left the kingdom, Uttanapada felt remorse for his action. He decided to bring him back and set out on the mission when Sage Narada came and pacified Uttanapada. "He will come back after achieving his goal," said Narada.

One day, Sage Narada came to the king and announced that Dhruva had attained the *darshan* of Sri Hari. The king was elated, so were the queens Suniti and Suruchi. Suruchi had also realised her fault. Uttanapada sent elephants, horses and chariots to escort little Dhruva back home. It was the most joyful reunion.

Dhruva succeeded his father to the throne and ruled for many years. At the time of his leaving this material world, Sri Hari sent two messengers and made him the Dhruva Tara (Pole Star), who would shine till the Universe existed.

Even today, we can see the Pole Star, shining happily as if immersed in the bliss of divine love for Sri Hari!

136. *Tulsi and Shankhachuda*

Goddess Vrinda is another name of Tulsi and her story is mentioned in the Brahmavaivarta Purana. Vrinda was the daughter of King Dharmadwaja. She married the demon-king Shankhachuda. Shankhachuda was born to the demon-king Dambha. Shankhachuda was, in fact, Sudama in his previous life. He was born in the family of demons due to the curse of Radha. When Shankhachuda grew up, he went to Pushkar and performed austere penance to please Brahma. Brahma blessed him and said that he would remain invincible. He also instructed Shankhachuda to go to Badrikashrama where he would find his would-be wife Tulsi, the daughter of Dharmadhwaja.

Shankhachuda went to Badrikashrama and married Tulsi. He then returned to his capital accompanied by his wife Tulsi. When Shankhachuda reached his capital after marrying Tulsi, he was crowned king of the demons. After his coronation, Shankhachuda attacked the devas and defeated them.

137. *Shankhachuda Rules*

In a very short time, all the three worlds were under Shankhachuda's control. After being defeated by Shankhachuda, the gods went to Brahma and sought his help. Brahma then took them to Vishnu. All of them were taken to Shiva by Vishnu. Shiva assured the gods that he would certainly kill Shankhachuda.

Shiva sent his messenger named Pushpadant to Shankhachuda to ask him to return the kingdom of the gods to them. Shankhachuda refused to oblige this demand. On the contrary, he expressed his willingness and readiness to fight Shiva.

Shiva first sent all his ganas under the leadership of Karttikeya and Ganesha. Later on, Bhadrakali proceeded towards the battlefield. At last, Shiva proceeded accompanied by the gods. All the troops collected at the bank of the river Chandrabhaga.

138. *Shiva Kills Shankhachuda*

A fierce battle ensured between the gods and the demons. After the defeat of the gods and the ganas, Karttikeya and Ganesha came forward to fight Shankhachuda. Later on, they were joined by Bhadrakali. Bhadrakali would have devoured Shankhachuda, but she spared his life because of the boon, given to him by Brahma. Now, it was the turn of Shiva to join the battle, but even he could not cause any harm to him because of Lord Brahma's boon. Vishnu appeared in the guise of a Brahmana and demanded the armour from Shankhachuda, which he had put on his body. Shankhachuda gave away his armour to him without any suspicion. Vishnu then went to Shankhachuda's wife in the guise of Shankhachuda. Tulsi, like a good and noble wife, embraced him without suspecting. Shankhachuda became furious and attacked Shiva. Shiva attacked him with his trishul or trident. Shankhachuda who had become powerless was killed instantaneously.

139. *Tulsi Curses Vishnu*

After being instructed by Parvati, Vishnu had gone to Tulsi in the guise of Shankhachuda so that Shiva could kill Shankhachuda. Initially, Tulsi could not recognise Vishnu. She was extremely joyous at her husband arrival. But very soon, she was able to realise the real identity of Vishnu, who had disguised himself as her husband. She became angry and cursed Vishnu to become a stone. She was crying unconsolably.

Vishnu contemplated on Shiva as a result of which he appeared. Shiva blessed Tulsi that she would become the beloved of Vishnu. Due to Tulsi's curse, Vishnu attained the form of Shaligram which is a stone. Because of Shiva's blessings, Tulsi leaves are offered to the Shaligram, in the process of its worship.

140. *Savitri and Satyavan*

The Brahmavaivarta Purana tells us the story of Savitri. In the kingdom of Bhadra, there lived a king named Ashwapati who had a beautiful daughter named Savitri. As she grew up, Savitri embarked on a journey to find a worthy groom.

Her wanderings led her to the Tapovan, where she encountered King Dyumatsen of Salva, who had lost his kingdom to an enemy. There, her eyes fell on his son, Satyavan, and decided he would be her husband. The gods had prophesied that he would die within a year. But Savitri was set on marrying Satyavan.

After marrying Satyavan, Savitri dutifully served her mother-in-law and father-in-law. As time passedby, the predicted day of Satyavan's death drew near. On the appointed day, as Satyavan went to the forest to gather firewood with Savitri by his side, he suddenly experienced excruciating pain in his head descended from a tree and lay dead.

141. *Savitri is Blessed with Boons*

Yama sent down his Yamadootas or messengers to fetch Satyavan. But Savitri refused to let him go. Yama himself appeared and tried to convince Savitri, explaining that it was the law of Nature. However, Savitri declined to accept his words and started following Yama. Moved by Savitri's unwavering loyalty and devotion to her husband, Yama said, "Ask for any boon you desire." Savitri made three requests: "Grant divine sight to my blind father-in-law and mother-in-law, and restore my father-in-law's kingdom," she pleaded. Yama granted her this wish. Finally, Savitri asked "Let me be the mother of a hundred sons of Satyavan." Touched by her unwavering dedication, Yama relented and revived Satyavan. Thus, Savitri and Satyavan ruled their kingdom happily ever after, experiencing eternal bliss and prosperity. Savitri-vrata is a Vrata or ritual to prevent a wife from ever getting widowed.

142. *Garuda and Aruna*

Sage Kashyapa had two wives – Kadru and Vinata. Once, Sage Kashyapa asked his wives to ask a boon each. Kadru asked for one thousand Nagas or serpents as her sons. Vinata wished for two sons who were greater in strength than the thousand sons of Kadru. Sage Kashyapa gave them the boons and asked to nurture the embryos with care.

In due course, Kadru gave birth to one thousand eggs and Vinata gave birth to two eggs. After several years, a thousand sons emerged from Kadru's eggs. But Vinata's eggs did not hatch yet. As days passed, Vinata grew impatient and she was also jealous of the sons of Kadru. So, out of curiosity she broke open one of her eggs in secret and a semi-grew child came out of it, which was Aruna, the charioteer of the Surya. Aruna thus enraged cursed his mother Vinata to be a slave of Kadru. Garuda hatched from the other egg.

143. *Garuda Brings Amrita*

Later, Aruna granted her the redemption from the curse that after five hundred years the other egg would hatch and a powerful son would be born out of it. "Garuda, your son will release you from the clutches of Kadru," Aruna said.

Vinata became Kadru's slave in contest to find out the colour of Indra's horse-tail. The former lost in the contest as Kadru's naga children hung on the tail of the horse. Originally, the colour of the tail was white, but Kadru tricked and won the contest.

By this time, five hundred years passed and the other egg hatched. Garuda came out with blazing effulgence, shone like Surya, and rose into the sky with incredible speed. Garuda was much worried about the serfdom of his mother and asked Kadru what he should do to release his mother. They demanded the Amrita which was under the control of Indra.

144. *Garuda Becomes Vishnu's Vahana*

After a lot of struggle with Indra in heaven, Garuda did manage to get some Amrita. As planned, Garuda gave the Amrita to Kadru and released his mother. Soon after, Indra took back the Amrita. Because of this victory, Vishnu gave him the permission to be his vahana. Therefore, Garuda became Vishnu's mount after this heroic encounter with Indra.

Garuda received a boon from Indra that he should be permitted to prey on snakes and to avenge the nagas for ill-treating his mother. The request was granted and thereupon, he went on preying on snakes.

"Enable me to compose a Purana of my own – the Garuda Purana," said Garuda. "So be it!" said Vishnu. Garuda taught his Purana to Sage Kashyapa. When the sage chanted its hymns, he could bring back a dead tree to life.

145. *Sage Ashtavakra's Marriage*

Sage Ashtavakra wanted to marry Suprabha, daughter of Sage Vadanya. Sage Vadanya agreed to the marriage but before that, Ashtavakra had to pass a test.

Ashtavakra should go to the Himalayas in the north to pay homage to Shiva and Parvati and further go north and talk to a beautiful woman residing there. When Ashtavakra returned successfully, he would win the hand of Suprabha in marriage.

Sage Ashtavakra accepted the challenge and he went north. First, he went to the palace of Kubera. He then went further north and had darshan of Shiva and Parvati.

He then went further north and met a beautiful woman named Uttara. The woman tried to entice Ashtavakra. But the Sage did not fall for her tricks. Finally, Uttara asked the Sage to marry her. Ashtavakra denied her request by saying that he was in love with Suprabha. She then blessed the Sage and helped him in his early return. Sage Ashtavakra successfully returned and married Suprabha.

146. *Sage Ritavak Curses a Star*

Towards the end of the tenure of the influence of the Revati star, a son was born to Sage Ritavak. Ritavak sought to bring up his son and teach him properly. But the son of the sage became evil-natured, and thus brought shame to the family. In despair, Sage Ritavak and his wife became upset and fell ill. The evil deeds of their son caused their mental suffering.

One day, frustrated with his son's misdeeds, Sage Ritavak asked Sage Garga, "I am a good-natured and dedicated Brahmana. Both I and my wife have followed a virtuous path of life. So, why has my son become evil-minded?" Garga said, "Since your son was born towards the close of the period under the power of Revati star, he has gone astray." In agony, Sage Ritavak cursed the Revati star– "Let you fall from the sky." Cursed by the sage, the star fell from the sky, upon Mount Kumuda on the earth.

147. *Mahishasura*

Rambha was the king of demons. Once, he saw a water buffalo and fell in love with her. So, he converted himself into a male water buffalo and started living with her. A son was born to them and they named him Mahisha.

Mahisha was an evil demon. He decided to pray to Brahma, who he thought would grant him a boon, which would make him invincible.

Mahishasura performed austere penances praying and fasting for months as he stood on one foot. Brahma was pleased with him and came to grant him a boon. Mahishasura asked for immortality. Brahma said that he could not have the boon of immortality as every creature that was born had to die. Mahishasura decided that he would ask for a boon that would make him as good as immortal. He asked that no man or god should be able to kill and, if he had to die, it should be only at the hands of a woman.

148. *Birth of Durga*

Having obtained the boon from Brahma, Mahishasura thought himself to be invincible. He and the other asuras went about hurting and killing everyone on the earth. Then they went to heaven to fight the gods. Even Indra's thunderbolt could not withstand their attack. Mahishasura drove out the gods and took over Indra's throne. Mahishasura started harassing all pious people who continued praying to Vishnu and Shiva. The gods and the people were distressed and decided to ask Shiva for help. Shiva, Vishnu, and Brahma concentrated hard and used their radiant energies, which were joined by the energies from Indra, and the other gods. The divine energy took the form of a divine lady with a thousand arms. This was Durga. Once, she was beautifully dressed, the gods armed her with all the weapons needed to kill the demons.

149. *Slaying of Mahishasura*

Vishnu gave her his Sudharshana Chakra, Shiva handed over his Trishul, and Brahma gifted her his Lotus along with his Kamandalam of holy water and wisdom. Finally, she was given a lion to sit on. With all the blessings from the gods, she mounted the lion and set out to do away with Mahishasura.

Mounted on the fiery lion, she roared ferribly. It was a roar that shook mountains and created huge waves in the seas. Even Mahishasura was worried for a second, but his vanity took over when he saw that the terrible form was that of a woman. Durga created a large army from her breath to fight Mahishasura's army and then fought with Mahishasura who came in the form of a buffalo. After a long duel, she killed him with her sword. Thus she freed the world from Mashishasura's evil doings.

150. *Karma Vipak*

Karma means the action and Vipak means the fruit one reaps according to his or her Karma. At Yamapuri, Chitragupta goes through the record of all the deeds, committed by a man when he was alive, and brings into the notice of Yama. Yama then decides upon the punishment to be given to the soul concerned. The souls of virtuous people are sent to heaven. Those who have extreme attachment to women take rebirth as human beings. People who have attained martyrdom while fighting a battle are sent to Indrapuri. Those who have engaged themselves in virtuous deeds throughout their lives are rewarded for their good deeds.

Sinners who have remained disinclined towards any kind of virtuous deed, or those who have abandoned their faithful wives, are sent to a hell named Raurav.

151. *Description of Hells*

Lord Brahma tells about different kinds of hells. Those who have illicit relationships or are in the company of sinners go to the first hell. Felling of trees and stealing the fruits of others' trees lead one to the second hell. People who kill creatures unworthy of killing and those who quarrel over property dispute go to the third hell.

Terrorising the living creatures and deviating from one's own religion lead one to the fourth hell. Behaving deceitfully with friends leads one to the fifth hell. Keeping somebody in captivity and causing hurdles in the path of others would lead one to the sixth hell. Stealing royal property leads one to the seventh hell. Greed and misuse of hard-earned money lead one to the eighth hell.

Stealing the Brahmana's property and condemning others lead one to the ninth hell. People who lack courtesy or who steal sacred texts go to the tenth hell. Thus, every creature, as per his/her deed, is sent to the hell of his/her own choice.